CITY GARDENING

PLANTING, MAINTAINING, AND DESIGNING THE URBAN GARDEN

DEIRDRE COLBY

KEN DRUSE, CONSULTING EDITOR
MARIA C. GLEASON, CONTRIBUTING EDITOR
HANS VAN ZELST, SPECIAL CONSULTANT

PRINCIPAL PHOTOGRAPHER
KEN DRUSE

Simon and Schuster

New York   London   Toronto   Sydney   Tokyo

A FRIEDMAN GROUP BOOK

Copyright © 1987 by Michael Friedman Publishing Group, Inc.

Simon and Schuster/Fireside Books,
Published by Simon & Schuster, Inc.
Simon & Schuster Building
Rockefeller Center
1230 Avenue of the Americas
New York, New York 10020

SIMON AND SCHUSTER, FIRESIDE and colophons are registered trademarks of
Simon & Schuster, Inc.

CITY GARDENING: Planting, Maintaining, and Designing the Urban Garden
was prepared and produced by
Michael Friedman Publishing Group, Inc.
15 West 26th Street
New York, New York 10010

Editor: Louise Quayle
Copy Editor: Mary Forsell
Art Director: Mary Moriarty
Designer: Robert W. Kosturko
Photo Editor: Philip Hawthorne
Production Manager: Karen L. Greenberg

Typeset by BPE Graphics, Inc.
Color separations by Hong Kong Scanner Craft Company Ltd.
Printed and bound in Hong Kong by Leefung-Asco Printers Ltd.

1 3 5 7 9 10 8 6 4 2
1 3 5 7 9 10 8 6 4 2 Pbk.

Library of Congress Cataloging in Publication Data

Colby, Deirdre.
    City gardening.

    "Fireside book."
    Bibliography: p.
    Includes index.
    1. Gardening.   2. Gardens—Design.   I. Druse,
Kenneth.   II. Gleason, Maria.   III. Van Zelst, Hans.
IV. Title.
SB453.C618   1987b   635.9   87-14866
ISBN 0-671-63697-9
ISBN 0-671-63698-7 (pbk.)

DEDICATION

From Pliny the Elder, to the present, this book is dedicated to
the literary tradition of garden writing. Thank you for the
inspiration and imagery that keep vibrant my visions of paradise.

ACKNOWLEDGMENTS

My grateful thanks for their time and expertise are due to:
Bonnie Billet, Bonnie Billet Horticulturists; Jane Brennan,
Assistant Librarian, New York Botanical Garden; Dimitri's
Gardens Ltd.; Josh Edgerly, New York Planter Co.; Susan
Rademacher Frey, Editor-in-Chief, Landscape Architecture &
Garden Design; Charlotte Frieze Jones, Springland
Associates; Lothian Lynas, Head Reference Librarian, New
York Botanical Garden; Cindy Olson, C.O.R.E. Contracting;
Leo Plofker, structural engineer; Pam Wilkinson, Managing
Editor, *American Gardens of the Nineteenth Century*, The
University of Massachusetts Press.
Thanks are also due to Roz Bernstein, Robert Colby, Kavid
Koosis, Susan Littlefield, Timothy Mawson, Edwin T. Morris,
Linda Reville, Marge Ternes, David Winn, and Linda Yang for
their encouragement and support. Thank you to Louise
Quayle, Philip Hawthorne, Sharon Kalman, Bob Kosturko,
and Karla Olson for invaluable advice, assistance, and
support. And a special thanks to Flora Stuart, whose magical
garden in Ocho Rios, Jamaica, West Indies, continues to be
an enduring source of enlightenment.

C O N T E N T S

CONTENTS

INTRODUCTION

No one would contest that the allure of trade and commerce has been one of the primary motivations for people around the world to leave their rural lifestyles for urban centers. Yet, increased commercial activity has never, and will never, replace the human need, for both aesthetic and health reasons, to be surrounded by beauty and nature. This is evidenced by the incorporation of public and private parks and gardens in even the most crowded spaces throughout the world.

For example, Paris, often called the most beautiful city in the world, was designed after the revolution to be a work of art, with its connecting grand boulevards lined with trees. However, its aesthetic design was inspired by the requirement of the people for refuge from the city—escape they found in lush growth and nature. Two game parks originally owned by the aristocracy were maintained, literally, for the kings of the people. They became the two infamous public parks flanking the city—Bois de Bologne in the east, and Parc Vincennes in the west.

Meanwhile, in North America, city squares were well shaded and many streets were tree lined. In

New York, the first public park, Bowling Green, was opened in 1733. However, the city was also filled with private gardens, usually in backyards.

In nineteenth-century America, a new movement inspired by Andrew Jackson Downing encouraged the development of naturalistic, ''picturesque'' gardens. As a result, the large urban park designed without an emphasis on formal design emerged as a new phenomenon. One such park is Central Park in New York City, designed by Olmsted and Vaux. The idea of the public park was pushed through by reformers for the therapeutic benefit of the increasing hordes of workers pouring into the cities. In this same spirit of adding nature to the urban landscape, the New York Botanical Garden was established in 1899.

Concerned that cities might spread haphazardly or harbor disease and infection, reformers instituted the City Beautiful Movement. The movement focused on integrating city functions with the beauty of nature. The reconstruction of San Francisco after the great earthquake, for example, incorporated many of these ideals with its grand Golden Gate Park.

By the nineteenth century in Europe, apartment living had become traditional in Paris, Vienna, Berlin, Prague, Warsaw, St. Petersburg, and Dresden. In London, Mr. & Mrs. John C. Louden began a journal to address a new interest in plantings for small spaces of an acre or less.

The invention of the electric motor and, subsequently the elevator, made tall apartment buildings possible. In the 1920's in New York, after the Park Avenue railroad tracks were covered, it was chic for society members to move into apartment buildings along both sides of the avenue. As a result, penthouses became part of sophisticated city living. Additionally, from the 1950's through the present, the terrace has come into its own as a way of giving some sense of the outdoors to apartment dwellers.

These developments, rather than diminishing the city garden, altered its specifications by moving the site upward. Since that time, urban gardens have continued to be adjusted to scale and perspective; however, their original purpose of providing aesthetic and physical respite has been maintained.

"The best way to survive life in the city," garden expert Ken Druse says, "is to have a way to get away from it: a bit of green, a patch of blue sky—contact with growing things. In order to experience the true benefit of a garden to soothe and restore the spirit, you don't need to have a rambling country house or to book a villa on the Mediterranean for three months in the summer. The power of nature is legion. A simple window box can remind you of beauty, growth, and the continuity of life on earth. There's nothing like it!"

Susan Rademacher Frey, editor-in-chief of *Landscape Architecture* and *Garden Design* magazines which are published by the American Society of Landscape Architects, suggests that the urban gardener should capitalize on the small garden space by making it very personal and expressive. "Spark an experience that mingles the intrinsic qualities of you and the place," she advises. "Look for something to respond to, even in the most desolate places. For instance, the view of a water tank might evoke country memories. . . . Garden design operates on two levels. Physically, it is total sensual engagement. Symbolically, it tells your story as it lives in that place. We want to be more fully alive. One way to recreate and reproduce ourselves is in a private garden. Metaphorically, in this same way, gardens can recreate the city.''

French landscape architect, Gilles Clement, agrees that a successful urban garden will not thrive unless its attendant is passionate and personal. ''A garden can't live unless it is loved by its owner,'' he says. ''You have to ask yourself, 'What is this plant? What is its significance?' Every plant has a soul.''

Yet, a great number of would-be city gardeners are intimidated by what they interpret as a new and unfamiliar set of cultivation rules. They do not recognize that the true basis for successful urban gardening is the same as for any kind of gardening. As Reginald Farrar, the late nineteenth century plant collector and rock-gardener defines it in *A Yorkshire Garden*, a successful gardener must be '' . . . a lover of his flowers, not a critic of them. I think the true gardener is the reverant servant of nature, not her truculent wife-beating master. I think the true gardener, the older he grows, should more and more develop a humble, grateful and un-

certain spirit, cocksure of nothing except the universality of beauty.''

Yet, this is not to say that special knowledge and skills are not necessary and should not be investigated before cultivating an urban garden. Frey stresses that a wealth of horticultural information on city gardening is available not only through horticultural societies, but also through other gardeners. She would like to see more linkage within the vast network of public, community, and private gardening and encourages the revitalization of public gardens. Ms. Frey emphasizes the differences between public parks and public gardens, saying, ''Public gardens express the soul of the community.'' Together, these garden spaces help define a city, and each garden adds a new and individual dimension.

Carrie Maher of the landscape architecture firm Maher & Greenwald, is responsible for some of New York's most impressive community garden efforts. The public garden at the Cathedral of St. John the Divine, for example, symbolically pays tribute to a number of religions. In doing so, it represents the diverse cultural identity of New York and successfully carries out Ms. Frey's requirement that a public space should reflect its community. A brick garden path is in the shape of a Celtic cross. Some of the plantings are arranged in a menorah-like design. The garden also makes visual references to the Tibetan Buddhist tradition and contains plantings revered in both North and South American sacred rituals.

Fruits and vegetables grown in this garden are used in meals for the needy and homeless. There is also a corps of underprivileged neighborhood kids for whom it is a badge of honor to belong to this great garden. They make it grow and often enjoy its fresh vegetables and fruits. The garden, therefore, not only represents, but also serves the community.

Classes for area school children who wish to learn more about how plants grow are conducted in nearby solar greenhouses. Outside, a variety of ancient flowers grow, laden with religious and mythical significance.

Many believe, as I do, that there should be legislation that designates spaces throughout cities as public or communal gardening plots. While free ground space is at a premium, a multitude of unused space exists above the ground, atop garages, and other relatively low buildings as well as on roofs of apartment houses. The low-weight-bearing capacity of some residential buildings is perhaps the single greatest obstacle to creating private city gardens. However, technological breakthroughs can compensate for this hindrance.

The artistic challenge for the urban gardener is to create a flourishing plot in very little space. Therefore, a city garden should have in quality what it lacks in quantity. This book adheres to this philosophy. Disheartened by the losing battle city dwellers often wage with vandalism and the inconsiderate public, I have chosen not to address frontyard city gardens and to concentrate on backyard, roof, penthouse, and terrace garden design. Principles for these gardens can be applied to frontyard spaces, however. Wherever your garden may be, you will succeed if you follow Ms. Maher's advice: "Let the garden be your teacher. Remember, the seeds you hold in the palm of your hand already know what to do."

CHAPTER ONE

THE URBAN ENVIRONMENT

CLIMATE AND HARDINESS ZONES

SOIL

CITY CODES AND WEIGHT RESTRICTIONS

BUDGETING

"Half the interest of a garden is the constant exercise of the imagination," wrote Mrs. C.W. Earle in 1897 in *Pot-Pourri from a Surrey Garden*. A creative art, designing and planning a garden should afford its owner as much pleasure as the final result. In fact, the more carefully you plan and design beforehand, the more successful your city garden will be.

Even though a terrace, a balcony, or an atrium can become another living room, gardening is more complicated than interior decorating; choosing plants, making beds, and maintaining soil conditions requires more effort than, for example, picking out a chair. Making a city garden is a creative, resourceful process of trial and error. Trees, shrubs, flowers, and vegetables are living creatures, and these "greenlings," like children and pets, need time and care. City living can be even more stressful for them than it is for us, and that's saying something! Aside from the obvious specter of pollution, one reason for this difficulty in adjusting is that they must adapt to an artificial habitat. Many of the more beloved popular selections for city gardens are not necessarily native to

Seeming to grow naturally and effortlessly, this informal Washington, D.C., garden is the product of careful planning.

Rhododendrons, peonies, and irises thrive in the full sun on this exposed rooftop.

nearby suburban or rural areas. It is useful to learn which trees and shrubs are indigenous to the immediate region, and a good atlas will provide a natural vegetation map of North America.

In alleys behind apartment buildings, and most especially on the balconies, terraces, and rooftops, a growing environment has to be simulated. One approach is to force a planting scheme on the garden—not an approach I would advocate, unless you want to work against nature. Such a process usually involves inordinate doctoring and altering to keep plants alive that are not native to or compatible with a particular region. This folly will demand time-consuming maintenance from either you or the expensive landscape-maintenance service you will need to hire. This is not to say that making adjustments and soliciting professional care won't be necessary. The recommended approach, however, is to design your garden based on the plants that will thrive on the strengths, weaknesses, and idiosyncracies of your particular growing conditions. If a plant is in an environment that won't support it, it will die.

CLIMATE AND HARDINESS ZONES

The amount of precipitation and the temperature range in your area constitute your local climate. The most important component that lets you know what you can grow in your area is *temperature*. *Hardiness* describes the lowest winter temperature at which a tree, shrub, or flower can survive. There are ten zones in the United States and Canada. The U.S.D.A. hardiness zone map (see right) shows the lowest average winter temperature in your zone. When choosing plants, use this chart as a guide to be sure you get the right plants for your climate. If you live in Louisville, Kentucky, for example, you live in Zone 6, and you may choose plant materials that are hardy to, or can survive, a minimum winter temperature of −10°F to 0°F (−23°C to −18°C). The last spring frost is between March 30 and April 30, and the first fall frost usually occurs between September 30 and October 30. Therefore, the average growing season in Louisville is 225 days.

Factors other than just latitude and longitude, however, affect hardiness. Cities that are along the same general latitude north, for example, may have milder or more severe climates than their counterparts. For example, Fargo, North Dakota, has an inland climate with hot summers and cold winters. On approximately the same latitude, Fargo's counterpart Vancouver, British Columbia, is a coastal city with a mild climate because of its location. Cities around the Great Lakes, on the other hand, are affected by lake-effect precipitation, while those along the Gulf Coast are subject to seasonable stormy weather. In a city such as Denver, Colorado, the high altitude also will have a bearing on what can be grown there. Wind-swept prairie states, on the other hand, have their own special climate, while in the American Southwest aridity is a factor. While climatic conditions vary widely, city gardens are thriving all over North America.

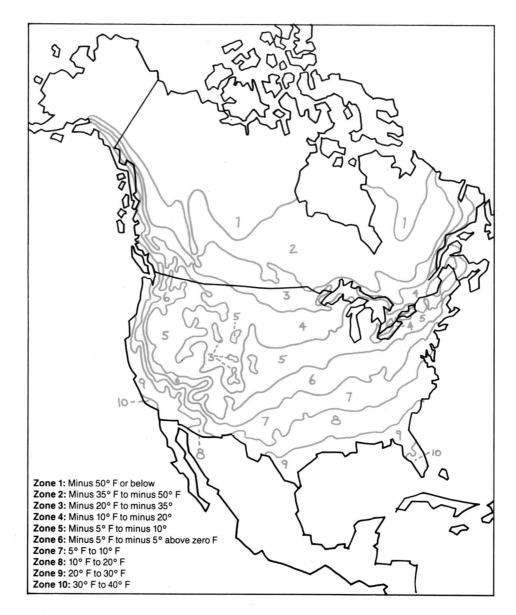

Zone 1: Minus 50° F or below
Zone 2: Minus 35° F to minus 50° F
Zone 3: Minus 20° F to minus 35°
Zone 4: Minus 10° F to minus 20°
Zone 5: Minus 5° F to minus 10°
Zone 6: Minus 5° F to minus 5° above zero F
Zone 7: 5° F to 10° F
Zone 8: 10° F to 20° F
Zone 9: 20° F to 30° F
Zone 10: 30° F to 40° F

Plant Hardiness Zone Map

Different types of plants and trees are only able to withstand a certain mean low temperature. Every city in North America belongs to one of ten growing zones; your garden selections must include only those plants that are suited to your city's zone.

Miniclimates

In addition to your regional climatic conditions, your garden space has its very own *miniclimate*, which includes the variables of sun, shade, moisture, and wind exposure. Together, these factors determine the optimum growing conditions for your city garden. Experienced urban gardeners know that they have to juggle what they want with what they can have.

If you have a sheltered backyard garden, low light levels will probably affect plant selection more than anything else. You might have only two to six hours of sun per day, which is considered partial shade. If you have less than two hours of sun you have full shade. In either case, you have a variety of plants to choose from that like shady growing conditions, such as flame azalea, periwinkle, and Canadian hemlock.

Garden walls that are painted or finished in light colors will reflect more light and warmth into your sheltered garden. Sheltered gardens can be warmer than surrounding areas in winter if they are protected from wind with a fence or hedge of evergreens or yews. Under these conditions, city gardeners could try some plants from one hardiness zone to the south of their own. For a different effect, if there are trees already on the property, you can "create" more light by removing some of the branches. This has an added bonus of increasing air circulation so that fungal problems can be prevented. Poor air circu-

© Derek Fell

This small, shady courtyard has been designed to make the most of what sunlight it does get and of its horizontal growing space.

lation in the sheltered garden will tend to keep soils damp and even boggy. There is, however, a range of plants, including tamarack trees, wintergreen shrubs, and marsh marigolds, that like very moist conditions. If the drainage is so poor that you practically have a swimming hole, there is much that a landscape contractor can do to improve the site.

Exposed sites, such as rooftops, penthouses, terraces, and balconies, often receive six to twelve hours of direct sunlight daily and perhaps additional indirect light as well. This seems to be the best of all possible situations; the range of flowering and vegetable-producing plants that can grow in these conditions is virtually unlimited. Too much sun and wind can be a problem, however. Plants bake in intense summer heat; excessive wind pulls moisture out of plants' leaves, causing them to wilt; and containers often freeze solid in winter. If your exposed site is windy, containers may have a tendency to topple if not weighted properly.

In exposed sites, most plants welcome a little shade from broiling sun, so that such overhead structural amenities as trellises, pergolas, slatted lathe houses, and shade trees are desirable additions. Fences and other vertical structures may help diminish the drying effects of wind. Awnings, canopies, and umbrellas are easily destroyed by strong rooftop winds, unless they are secured or located in a protected spot.

Depending on which way they face (north, south, east, or west), terraces, balconies, and penthouses generally are exposed some of the time and shaded part of the time. A south-facing terrace usually gets sunlight practically all day long and offers the widest growing selection of fruits, vegetables, and flowers. East- and west-facing terraces receive about six hours of sunshine, but in the morning and afternoon, respectively. Because of cooler morning sun, hydrangeas, daylilies, impatiens, and azaleas are good plants for east-facing balconies. West-facing balconies, which receive warmer afternoon light, can sport privet,

A rose collection surrounds a breakfast nook on a wraparound terrace. Designed by Lisa Stamm.

© Ken Druse

geraniums, coreopsis, roses, and herbs. A north-facing exposure receives the least sunlight, perhaps as little as two hours a day. Although the city gardener with a north-facing exposure might face a greater challenge in plant cultivation, a magnificent garden can be created with a broad variety of plant materials to choose from, such as begonias, hostas, ferns, and some forms of the colorful rhododendron.

Within your site, too, plantings may vary due to the influences of light and shade. A penthouse terrace may wrap around two or three sides of a building. In fact, neighboring buildings can affect sun and shade patterns by cutting off sunshine or reflecting more of it to you from light-colored walls and windows. Heat, too,

can be reflected from neighboring buildings, and in some cases it is absorbed during the day and radiated back to the garden at night. This can be a boon to the cool north-facing exposure and a bane to a sultry southern one.

If it is very windy on one or both sides of your garden in the sky, you may have to provide shelter by erecting latticed partitions on which vines like honeysuckle can be grown to create a windbreak. Dense shrubs such as yew also can act as protective screens and windbreaks. Many landscape experts advise city gardeners to select plants from one or two hardiness zones north of their own because of adverse windy conditions on roofs, balconies, and terraces.

This little garden has an eastern exposure, therefore it gets cooler morning sun.

Depending on your climate and miniclimate, you may have a perfect spot for a tiny lily pond stocked with goldfish.

Zeroing in on Your Miniclimate

Whenever you have a chance—spring, summer, fall, or even winter—the key to discovering your miniclimate is observation. Draw a simple diagram of your garden and note where the sun hits it at various points in the day, how precipitation drains, and other important natural features as outlined.

1. Note which direction your site faces and whether you receive partial shade, full shade, direct sunlight, or some form of indirect sunlight. Determine where it is sunniest and for how long. Note whether it is morning or afternoon sun. Observe when, and for how long, shadows fall.

2. When it rains, note how precipitation is distributed. You may see some areas getting soaking wet, other spots receiving less water, and some places—such as a fully sheltered corner—remaining almost completely dry.

3. Observe the direction and strength of the wind patterns. Garden photographer and writer Ken Druse suggests walking around on a windy day with a child's pinwheel to help figure it out. Find out where the wind is strongest and where it is calmest. Note how nearby buildings and such architectural elements as chimneys, buttresses, walls, and fences on and around your location affect the wind flow onto the site. Determine if there are changes in wind direction from summer to winter. You want to ensure that wind will not unexpectedly blow rain under awnings and into other sheltered spots. On the other hand, perhaps you will discover that your garden has almost no wind circulation.

Your diagram should serve as a general guideline based on your observation. Have some fun—exact knowledge of earth science isn't necessary! Your garden is unique and there's no better way to learn about your growing conditions than by firsthand experience. The reward is well worth the initial investment of your time and observation. By creating a garden that can live with you, you'll be making a garden you can live with: a permanent inspiration.

The United States Department of Agriculture's Extension Service and in Canada your provincial office of Agriculture Canada (see "Sources and Useful Addresses") offers a wealth of horticultural information. They are very comprehensive sources of information about the most pollution-tolerant and best-suited plantings for your city. Search out horticultural societies and garden clubs in your area. Quiz the person at the nursery. Most urban gardeners share information generously.

SOIL

For gardens on the ground, you will need to know the pH level, drainage capacity, nutrient and trace-element levels, and the balance between organic and inorganic matter in the soil. Most soil is composed of three substances: clay, sand, and organic matter. Any soil that has too much or too little of these ingredients has an imbalance.

Clay is made up of tiny, densely packed particles. It provides a secure foundation for plants, but if used alone, holds too much water and drowns plants. *Sand* is made up of relatively large particles. It provides excellent drainage and air circulation. But sandy soil has so many air spaces that water and nutrients run through too quickly. Roots therefore cannot absorb enough moisture and food. *Humus* is decayed material, such as leaf mold, dehydrated manure, or sphagnum peat moss. Humus helps soil retain water and nutrients. However, humus by itself retains too much moisture. When soil has a good balance of clay, sand, and humus, it is called *loam*—the gardener's best friend.

The acidity or alkalinity of soil also has to be in balance. The *pH acidity/alkalinity scale* ranges from 0 (most acid) to 14 (most alkaline). A pH of 7 is neutral. For most plants, 6.5 to 7 is optimum. However, many plants like a slightly acidic soil of 5.5 to 6.5 pH. Some plants, such as colorful azaleas and rhododendrons, thrive in acidic conditions. Others, like clematis, like it slightly alkaline.

There are two ways to learn something about the drainage on your property. Dig a hole one foot deep, fill it with water, and watch how quickly it drains away. If it drains too slowly, you may have too much clay. If the water disappears almost immediately, you may have sandy soil. A second way is to watch where the water goes during a heavy rainstorm. Does it run onto your neighbor's property or into your basement? Are there some areas that stay wet while others drain quickly? If there is a severe problem, you may need a landscape contractor to assess the situation—he can determine if the problem is one of slope, poor soil, or both.

Soil testing is necessary to determine pH levels, as well as quantities of nutrients, trace elements, and organic and inorganic matter in your soil. There are home-testing kits. However, the best way to ascertain soil makeup is to have it analyzed by a county extension agency, usually affiliated with a state university, or local office of Agriculture Canada.

"Soil testing is nothing more than an inventory of what is in the soil at the time the sample is taken," writes Ralph Snodsmith in his helpful *Tips from the Garden Hotline*. For a composite sample, gather about four cupfuls from all over the property. Remove any noticeable trash or rubble, then dig down 6 to 8 inches (15 to 20 centimeters) for the specimen. Place the soil in an airtight, sturdy container and attach a five-item note to the sample with the following information and requests:

1. Write down anything you know about what grew on the site before.
2. Request a trace-element test.
3. Briefly outline what you would like to grow, and ask whether or not your scheme is viable.
4. Ask how you can correct or amend the soil.
5. Ask what would grow best in the soil.

Mail the sample off in a sturdy container or airtight plastic bag in a padded envelope to your county extension agency or in Canada to the University of Guelph, Ontario or the Oric Garden Centre in Toronto (see "Sources" for addresses).

The charges for soil testing vary, but it is not expensive and worth every penny. The soil-testing service will tell you just about everything there is to know about your soil. You'll find out which nutrients it has or lacks, its composition and texture, and if

Sparkling clematis prefers alkaline soil and some shade.

Colorful rhododendron, perhaps the quintessential city shrub, requires slightly acidic soil.

Above left: *Brightly colored, fragrant Iceland poppies thrive in sunny spots throughout North America.* ***Above right:*** *This garden, consisting entirely of raised beds, includes one full of herbs and leafy green vegetables.*

any diseases or fungi are present.

Contingent upon the test results, you may be able to improve the quality of your old soil. Soils that have a high clay content can be loosened by the addition of gypsum or coarse builder's sand. Sandy soils improve when mixed with topsoil. Soil amendment also involves adding nutrients and fertilizers (see page 29). However, all soils improve with the addition of humus. Sphagnum peat moss is a good choice of humus. This coarse-textured organic material comes from bogs in Canada.

Acidic soils are commonly found in woodland and rainy areas. Overly acidic soil conditions can be corrected by adding ground limestone. Alkaline soils occur in arid areas and parts of the continent where surface limestone is present. Alkalinity may be adjusted a bit by adding humus. You may need something stronger if you live in the arid Southwest. If so, add sulfur according to the manufacturer's directions.

Sand, topsoil, sphagnum peat moss, ground limestone, and sulfur are available at garden centers. Ask the staff's opinion on how much of these additives to use and which tools you'll need. Generally, soil is best amended in the fall so that nutrients and additives have a chance to become integrated over the winter. Also, you'll have more time without being distracted by spring and summer chores.

If your soil is in very bad shape (filled with construction rubble, for example), you may have to prepare a raised bed of entirely new soil. A raised bed is simply a contained area for planting. Landscape, lighting, and irrigation designer Hans Van Zelst suggests the following raised bed construction:

1. Contain the bed with sturdy retaining walls of bricks, or tiles, railroad ties, or preserved wood about 20 inches (50 centimeters) high. Ultimately, the size of the bed depends on the size of your garden. An arrangement of stones reminiscent of New England's rock walls with violas poking out of the crevices would look lovely. You can frame the bed with anything, as long as the construction can contain the weight of the soil and the pressure of spreading root systems. If you encase the bed with stout redwood or cedar, you might think about planing its surface off with a bench for grandstand garden seating.

2. Put 2 to 3 inches (5 to 7.5 centimeters) of gravel on the bottom.

3. Cover the gravel with thin hairlike fiberglass netting (Dupont's Landscape Fabric or DeWitt's Weed Barrier, for example), which are easily found at a good nursery.

4. On top of the netting, lay 18 inches (45 centimeters) of topsoil mixed with 6 inches (15 centimeters) of sphagnum peat moss, or three parts topsoil to one part moss.

5. Add fertilizer suited to what you will be growing (see page 31).

A raised bed is just a giant container for soil. It gives you a fresh start and lets you influence the destiny of your plants.

CITY CODES AND WEIGHT RESTRICTIONS

*B*efore you begin any kind of city garden, inquire about your city's building and zoning codes. Generally, these are available from your city's building department. Obtain a written copy to be able to refer to as necessary. Make sure that you can recognize fire hazards and that you understand weight restrictions. Follow them exactly.

The weight restriction on roofs, penthouses, terraces, and balconies in older buildings in New York City, for example, is 40 pounds (18 kilograms) per square foot (0.09 square meter). In newer buildings, the weight restriction is reduced to 30 pounds (13 kilograms) per square foot. In cities where snowfall amounts are larger, the weight allowance may be 50 pounds (22 kilograms) per square foot, while in more southern cities it is not uncommon to find restrictions of as little as 20 (9 kilograms) or even 10 pounds (4.5 kilograms) per square foot.

When planning a large elevated city garden it is always advisable to contact a structural engineer. An engineer can best counsel you on a surface's structural soundness, alert you to which areas can tolerate the greatest and least amount of weight, and tell you what measures can be taken to distribute weight evenly. If surface conditions are poor, dunnage, or a deck, may have to be constructed to distribute the weight of a container garden. Many larger apartment buildings retain a structural engineer. If yours does not, call or write the local Association of Consulting Engineers or the group's headquarters in Washington, D.C., or Ottawa, Ontario. They may be able to answer your questions.

Drainage requirements and provisions should be provided by your landlord or building management company. In many places, building permits are required. In any case, speak to your landlord before assembling any container-supporting system on a roof, penthouse, or terrace. If the landlord or tenants' association offers resistance to your plans, point out that a well-landscaped terrace apartment can command a higher rental or selling price. And show them this book. Let them see how gorgeous and trouble-free a carefully constructed city garden can be.

Before this lush roof garden was designed, weight restrictions and drainage requirements were carefully studied.

BUDGETING

*D*epending on your resources, a sensible strategy is to think big but start small, expanding every year. Substantial city gardening is seldom inexpensive. City rents for garden-supply centers are high. Consequently, their prices are high, and their space and resources could be limited. In addition, the services of landscape professionals are not cheap. Start your garden with a small selection of plants, particularly trees and evergreen shrubs. Quality, rather than quantity, is the key. It is preferable to add to your design every year rather than to buy everything all at once if it means establishing a big, flashy garden with shoddy workmanship and inferior materials. Second-rate gardens inevitably have to be replaced.

Setting up a garden can involve lifting, stooping, and moving around some heavy materials. Think about whether you'll need help. It can be a good investment in your health—as well as in your garden—to hire a landscaping service to help out.

Basic Gardening Tools

If you're new to gardening, or just want to update your supplies, this list of tools covers the essential items necessary for maintaining a garden.

1. A **hose** with a spray attachment is a must for watering plants and also can be used to spray debris off paved surfaces.

2. A **rake** will facilitate clearing uprooted weeds, fallen leaves, and other unwanted waste in your garden.

3. A **pail** can be used for anything from carting weeds out of the garden to transporting fertilizer and soil.

4. A **hand-spading fork** is a good tool for turning soil and lifting a plant out of its growing spot for transplanting.

5. A **trowel** with a short or long handle is a gardener's staple used for light digging, transplanting smaller plants, and weeding.

6. **Pruning shears** facilitate clipping unwanted tree branches and cutting flowers. A heavy duty electric **hedge trimmer,** however, should be used for shaping and pruning larger bushes and trees.

7. **Gardening gloves** will protect your hands from injury and dirt, and a broad brimmed **hat** is ideal for keeping the hot sun out of your eyes and off of your head and neck.

8. A reversible **garden stool and kneeling pad,** which folds for easy storage, will save your body from some unnecessary aches and pains.

9. A small **hand truck or dolly** (available from larger hardware stores) is indispensable for transporting soil, weeds, or whatever to the street for disposal or from one part of your garden to another.

10. A small **shovel** will make heavy digging jobs easier.

Begin with a few tools and garden supplies, adding new ones as you need them. Storage space, too, is probably at a premium, so think about where you're going to stash something before you order or buy it.

© Ken Druse

CHAPTER TWO

PLANTING, PROCEDURES, AND MAINTENANCE

PLANTING

TROUBLE-SHOOTING

GARDEN CARE

CONTAINER GARDENING

DRIP IRRIGATION SYSTEMS

Once you have assessed the needs and condition of your site, you will need to decide on a planting scheme and plan a timetable of garden care, from ordering plants to winterizing beds. You must also determine what kind of garden will grow best for you, one that grows in a container or window box, one that blossoms from a soil bed, or any combination of these growing methods.

Additionally, a thorough understanding of the possible pitfalls you will face as an urban gardener is necessary to ensure long-term success. A consultation with a local expert, such as a horticulturist or your county or provincial agricultural agent will also help you determine which plants and garden-care methods will work best for you. Whatever planting scheme you choose for your garden, the basic procedures outlined in this chapter will help you get started.

Above right: The planting scheme for this corner of annuals can be changed every year. Red salvia, impatiens, marigolds, gladioli, and pink, flowering tobacco adorn the spot here. *Below right:* Every bit of horizontal growing space is being utilized on this colorful, narrow terrace, but there is no sense of overcrowding because of the even spaces between each planting.

PLANTING

A planting scheme can be scaled to a large or a small garden.

Ready for transplanting, this tree has just arrived from the nursery. Choose trees with root balls that are about as wide as the tree branches extend.

Trees, shrubs, flowers, fruits, and vegetables come ready to plant in several forms. Trees and shrubs tend to survive the best when they have been *balled and burlapped*. This simply means that their root balls are surrounded by soil that is wrapped up in burlap and tied with cord near the crown, where the trunk and roots meet. It's the least traumatic way for a middle-size tree or shrub to make the transition from the nursery to your city garden. Middle-size trees and shrubs measure between five and seven feet tall and have had a good start, even before you plant them. Planting instructions are usually included with your purchase. Also keep in mind that some trees have to be staked at first until they are strong enough to grow on their own.

Another planting method for smaller shrubs, dwarfed trees, and perennials from 2 to 6 feet high (1.9 to 5.4 meters) is *bare root*. Your selection arrives in a dormant state with its roots bare. Bare-root plants take longer to establish themselves than the balled-and-burlapped variety and can be harmed by windy terrace conditions. Follow the planting directions accompanying the selection. If you can't put the plant into the ground or a container right away, moisten the roots frequently to keep them from drying out.

Bulbs, such as crocuses, daffodils, and other annuals and many kinds of vegetables, fruits, and herbs can be grown from seedlings and carefully transplanted into your garden. Many herbs and vegetables can also be grown from seed. A lot of seeds come in one tiny packet. In small-space gardens, it is always better to use lesser amounts than the package directions suggest. If you want to get an early start, buy a seed-starter kit and germinate them indoors before planting them outdoors in the spring.

Generally, when you live in a cold climate, it is preferable to plant your garden in spring right after the last frost. This way, plant roots will be well established by winter. In areas with shorter, less severe winters, you can plant in the spring or in the fall before the ground freezes. Additionally, spring-flowering bulbs like tulips and hyacinths have to be planted in fall. Most herbaceous perennials like spring planting, but there are exceptions, as with peonies and Oriental poppies. In warm climates you can generally plant throughout the year, but no plants should be planted at the height of summer's heat.

Above: *City nurseries may offer only a limited selection of plants and supplies because they lack space. If you cannot find what you are looking for, try a nearby suburban nursery.*

It is a good policy to place your orders early because mail-order nurseries do run out of stock. Reputable suppliers send orders at the appropriate time for planting in your area, though you may be allowed to request a specific delivery date. If your order arrives while the ground is still frozen, well in advance of the planting date, send it back. Don't be too surprised if the shrub you have ordered isn't quite as pretty as the one pictured in the catalog. Catalogs usually depict perfect specimens photographed at maturity. However, if the plant has obviously been damaged in transit, refuse delivery and send it back.

An advantage in using catalogs is that they supply common names of plants along with their Latin botanical names. Common names vary from place to place, but Latin names are the same worldwide so you will always be able to identify the plant you want. Catalog descriptions often include information about hardiness zones, types of soil in which to plant, and sunlight requirements, which is generally all the information you need. A disadvantage when you order by mail, however, is that you have no choice in the appearance of what is being shipped to you. Trees and shrubs form the backbone of your garden: Their woody stems or evergreen boughs must complement your garden's design through every season. Therefore, I recommend that you pick them out from the local nursery. If you don't like its selection, or if it doesn't carry a particular item you're searching for, find a friend with a car, or rent one for the day, and drive out to a suburban nursery. Before you go, call ahead to make sure the one you visit has what you're looking for and can deliver larger orders to you in the city. Measure doors and elevators to make sure your new garden trees and shrubs won't be too tall or wide to squeeze through with a little bit of coaxing.

Be fussy and use your artist's eye. Van Gogh was inspired by the cypress tree. In his diary, the painter wrote that the tree "is as beautiful in line and proportion as an Egyptian obelisk" (Van Gogh at St. Rémy and Auvers. Metropolitan Museum of Art: New York, 1986). Select trees and shrubs for their interesting shapes, beautiful forms, or perfect symmetry. Look for richness and variation in the color of the bark and a pleasing configuration of branches.

Planting Vegetables

Cabbage, spinach, onions, cauliflower, beets, peas, lettuce, and asparagus are cool-season vegetables. They require an outdoor growing temperature of 48°F to 70°F (8°C to 21°C). Parsley, chicory, and chives also enjoy early planting. (Consult package directions for each plant's specific sowing timetable, and the frost date map for your growing season.)

Such warm-season vegetables as beans, eggplant, peppers, tomatoes, and summer squash need day and night-time temperatures between 55°F and 90°F (12°C and 32°C). They should be planted when all danger of frost has passed, about two weeks after leaves have appeared on the trees. In spring, if your garden is threatened by a late frost, insulate budding plants by covering them with heavy-duty plastic garbage bags. Warm-season herbs—which are mostly annuals and include basil, caraway, chervil, coriander, sweet marjoram, and arugula—should also be planted when all possibility of frost has passed.

Ordering Plants

On a cold January evening, seed catalogs are a thrilling reminder that spring is just around the corner. It's impossible to plant in winter, but it's a wonderful time to plan. Our imaginations have more space than our city gardens, so think about your design as you read through, and try to resist the temptation to send away for everything you see.

© Derek Fell

Succulent tomatoes and green peppers allowed to ripen until they are red and sweet are but two of the rewards of an urban vegetable garden.

TROUBLE⋈SHOOTING

Regular watering is the number one priority for the maintenance of a flourishing city garden.

Here is a nice fat tomato horn worm, hard at work destroying tomatoes.

Despite your noblest intentions, it is inevitable that a plant that is supposed to flourish in your growing conditions just won't do so. It may have been a weak or unhealthy specimen in the first place. If you wish to replant the specimen in the same spot, try investigating the possible reasons why the plant did not grow. Perhaps the soil has been drying out too quickly or staying too wet. The amount of sunlight may have been too little or too much. In these cases, try replanting in another spot. If you still don't get good results, this just may not be the right plant for the site.

While there are fewer pests in city gardens than in rural sites, you will undoubtedly encounter a few. The indomitable red spider is said to have been seen crawling up the Empire State Building in New York City in January! Aphids, caterpillars, and white flies are the most common garden pests. When insects or diseases are responsible for a plant's demise, there are recognizable signs. Curled, dry leaves, holes, and ragged edges usually indicate that a plant is under siege. Some insect is definitely responsible for any sticky substance above leaves or silvery webs below. Vegetables tend to be more susceptible to pests. Usually, a thorough spraying with insecticidal soap (read the label and follow directions) will get rid of common pests. Western Publishing Company's illustrated *Golden Guide to Insect Pests* is a handy reference book for identification. Other signs that a plant is sick include leaf rust (a disease resembling the familiar oxidant), leaf spot, and a thin coating of white, powdery mildew. Signs of root rot or water mold are more difficult to detect but manifest themselves in dry, wilting leaves, even though the soil is moist.

The best way to fight trouble is to identify the enemy. Pick off a few leaves, twigs, or dead bugs, stick them in a plastic bag, and show them to your nurseryman. If powerful insecticides are called for, read the label and follow directions. Insecticides are poisonous, so handle them with care and keep them away from children and pets. Personally, I would hire a certified insecticide applicator to do the job. Call your local botanical garden or horticultural society for references.

Finally, it is absolutely crucial that the garden is watered regularly during the growing season. A drip irrigation system (see page 37) is the most effective means of preventing over- or underwatering. Every so often, spray leaves to rid them of accumulated soot and grime or pests trying to get a foothold. If you are fortunate enough to have an area of lawn in your city garden, use a sprinkler system when needed from early spring to late fall.

GARDEN CARE

Feeding

City gardens, which grow in all kinds of soil mixtures, are particularly vulnerable to damage from an imbalance or lack of nutrients. Of all the nutrients required, nitrogen, phosphorous, and potassium are the most important. These elements are abbreviated on fertilizer bags as N, P, and K respectively. Nitrogen promotes vigorous green-foliage growth and overall vigor. Phosphorous stimulates flower production. Potassium—also called potash—is essential for sturdy stem and root growth and enhances both winter hardiness and immunity to diseases.

Chemical, inorganic fertilizers list the ingredients in order of nitrogen, phosphorous, and potassium. A good general N-P-K ratio is 5 percent, 10 percent, and 5 percent, respectively, which is written as 5-10-5. However, garden-center shelves are filled with fertilizers formulated just for evergreens, roses, azaleas, bulbs, vegetables, and many other kinds of plants. They are available in liquid, tablet, and granular forms.

Calcium, which strengthens cell walls, and magnesium, which aids in the process of photosynthesis, are also important. Additionally, there are seven less important elements that are known to be essential to plants' biochemical processes: boron, copper, iron, manganese, molybdenum, sulfur, and zinc. They are most readily found in organic fertilizers such as fish emulsion, bone meal, and dehydrated manure.

In New York City, the Bronx Zoo has kindly dehydrated and packaged animal manure, selling it as Zoo Doo. The Metro Toronto Zoo also packages the manure. It is available in nurseries in metropolitan areas. Check your local nursery to see if there is a similar initiative in your area.

Opinions vary on how frequently to fertilize. Landscape experts agree that plant food must be applied at least once in spring and then again in fall. One of the best guides is simply how healthy and green the plants are looking. Mr. Van Zelst recommends adding small, weekly doses of fish emulsion in a 5-1-1 ratio of N, P, and K all summer long. It seems to intensify flower colors and won't burn roots like the overuse of chemical fertilizers can. Whenever you are going to apply fertilizer, make sure you read the label and follow directions. However, many gardeners suggest erring on the conservative side.

Grass clippings (above) and wood chips (below) are two of the many possible types of mulch.

Mulching

A mulch is a layer of added material that covers the top of the growing medium in beds and containers. Mulching performs several vital functions. It helps to retard moisture evaporation from the soil—always a concern in container gardening. Mulching also smothers weeds by denying them access to sunlight. At the same time, mulch insulates the soil so that it maintains an even temperature, which is especially important in colder weather. By stabilizing soil temperature, the damage plants undergo from thawing and freezing in late winter is reduced.

Balsam boughs are a good choice for a supplemental mulch when laid over the autumn mulch about January 1 (a perfect use for the Christmas tree). Good choices for spring city garden mulches are aged minichips of bark. Straw is excellent for vegetable gardens. Mulches are usually applied twice a year. Apply them first in spring and then again in autumn after weeds and debris have been cleared away.

Weeding

Carefully consider each cut before you prune anything; a mistake will be very obvious to you for a long time.

If something is growing that you don't recognize, it could be a weed. However, do not be too quick to eliminate the plant. It may bloom into an attractive specimen. Ken Druse says, "A weed is an unwanted plant in an undesirable place. One person's weed is another's wildflower." Confirmed weeds should be eradicated as quickly as possible, however, because their growth can damage other plants. When the soil is wet, digging them out is easier. At the end of the growing season, it is always a good idea to thoroughly inspect the garden for any intruders. Western Publishing's illustrated *Golden Guide to Weeds* can help identify common culprits. If you are still uncertain about what a plant is or how to best get rid of it, bag a sample and take it to your local nursery for identification and advice on elimination.

Pruning

Pruning is the process of cutting something back. It could be the new growth at the top of a plant or the roots below the soil. Form and silhouette should be considered when pruning. Nothing in the garden is sorrier looking than a wretchedly hacked tree. Since special tools and a light touch are needed to properly perform this job, it might be best to hire a landscaping service to do it. However, you should be able to take care of the smaller plants and shrubs.

Root pruning is advisable when you suspect that a larger plant's roots are outgrowing its container home. A simple method involves plunging a spade directly into the growing medium, about two inches from the planter's edge, and scraping once or twice all the way around. A trowel works well for plants in small containers.

It is a good practice to remove flowers from plants as soon as they begin to fade. *Deadheading*, as this technique is called, promotes a longer flowering time, and keeps your garden looking neat and vibrant.

Winterizing

To prepare your garden for winter, pull weeds, throw out annuals, and eliminate sick or weak plants. Do a general cleanup. If your terrace is very windy, tuck lighter containers out of the wind. Plants in heavier tubs that are difficult to move may have to be staked with a cylindrical windscreen of burlap. Do this also with broadleaved evergreens such as holly and rhododendron if they are in very exposed sites. Furthermore, the leaves of all evergreens and conifers would do well to be protected with an antidessicant spray. Spray the plants again in midwinter to make sure they survive the winter.

With diligent pruning, espaliered shrubs and trees can be the most interesting features of a city garden and can soften an unornamented wall.

CONTAINER GARDENING

When you create a garden on a rooftop, terrace, or balcony, all your plantings will have to be in containers. Rather than being a limitation, however, container gardening offers you the opportunity to exercise your imagination. From a colorful African pot to an ornate sarcophagus, a container can be almost anything you choose, providing it conforms to certain criteria. Anything you select has to be light enough to satisfy weight restrictions on roofs, terraces, and balconies. (Never use soil alone—1 inch (2.5 centimeters) of topsoil weighs 100 pounds (45 kilograms) on a roof.) On older roofs, use lightweight containers. Containers have to be roomy enough for the roots of your chosen plants to grow. They have to be able to last through the coldest days of winter and the hottest days of summer. They also have to be able to tolerate being in contact with the constant moisture and must have holes in the bottom for drainage.

No container should ever lie directly on a surface. Elevate it 2 to 3 inches (5 to 7.5 centimeters) on bricks, pressure-treated wood blocks, or rollers, for adequate drainage. Be sure, too, not to push plants directly against a parapet wall. This could have the effect of making the plant grow in one direction. Leave about 3 inches (7.6 centimeters) between the plant and the wall for this reason, and so you can sweep away debris from behind the containers.

The larger the plant and the longer it lives, the more expansive its root system will be. A container must be matched with a plant's size. Trees, of course, need the largest containers. Shrubs (roses, taxus, and forsythia) and herbaceous perennials (asters, chrysanthemums, and daylilies) bloom every year, and their roots hibernate during the cold season. They require roomy, sturdy boxes and tubs. Planters for trees and shrubs also have to be rugged enough to withstand pressure from expanding roots without cracking. Trees and shrubs are long lived, so they need stalwart containers that can last for many winters. Because they bloom and die within one growing season, annuals (mari-

A colorful grouping of richly toned terra-cotta pots filled with a profusion of blooming flowers and small trees demonstrates the endless variations that can be created using containers.

Pots and tubs transform this rooftop into a lush retreat. Their positioning along the roof's edges and walls both defines the garden room and masks weatherworn sufaces. Additionally, their portability allows for easy seasonal changes and rearrangements.

golds, petunias, and snapdragons) can be grown in less durable containers.

Because the tannic acid in the wood keeps them from rotting, the most permanent containers are boxes and tubs made of redwood, cedar, teak, and mahogany. (If you want to use another kind of wood, such as yellow pine, make sure it has been pressure-treated with a preservative that is not toxic to plants.) If well constructed and properly maintained, containers can last for more than ten years. Ideally, the boxes should be reinforced along the exterior corners with aluminum, copper, or brass

brackets bolted in place. Anything larger than four or five feet long by two feet wide tends to be unwieldly. Sagging in the middle of a long trough can be alleviated by adding interior bracing to stabilize the construction. To prevent drooping, planters have to be supported from underneath with bricks or blocks.

A very durable and less expensive container is the ubiquitous whiskey half-barrel made of oak. For best results, it should be treated with copper or zinc napthanate, which is nontoxic to plants but should be used with caution nonetheless (read the

label and follow directions). Also, the metal hoops should be coated with Rustoleum™.

Elegant carved stone urns—Georgian, Regency, and Adamesque planting troughs—once found in stately European gardens are now being replicated in lighter weight materials such as fiberglass. Fiberglass copies of the dignified Versailles planting box—standing on four legs with finials atop each corner—are available through mail-order suppliers (see "Sources and Useful Addresses") Victorian cast-iron garden furniture and other classic lead forms—now hard to locate and unsuitably heavy for elevated gardens—are being realistically duplicated in aluminum. Old-fashioned planters decorated with garlands, leaf patterns, scrolls, and mythological creatures are expertly reproduced in weatherproof, lightweight materials. For rooftop rock gardens, rough-hewn pumice and simulated-stone alpine boxes are available.

Undeniably, planters and containers can provide interest in and of themselves. There are many exquisite Oriental urns and pots that can grace the city garden. You can look for something special at an auction house or in an art gallery. To protect your treasure, pot the plant first in an inexpensive container. For adequate drainage, the inner pot should sit on a few inches of gravel.

There are several styles of lightweight, imitation terra-cotta containers made of plastic that resemble their heavier counterparts (see page 33). Many, adorned with friezes and fluted mouldings, can fool even the most discerning eye. Make sure that terra-cotta pots, real or simulated, are frostproof.

Unattractive plastic containers can be covered with trailing plants and are perfect when used for cascades of flowering plants. In Italy, some inventive city gardeners wrap their containers in colorfast fabrics that complement their design schemes. Imagine pots of bushy, blue hydrangeas draped in a subtle pink and cream cotton design gracing the perimeter of a Florentine terrace. Use your imagination to invent other decorative motifs for containers, such as stenciling your own designs on your more unattractive pots.

Because of windy conditions on rooftops, hanging baskets are only appropriate in sheltered, backyard gardens. There are, however, many pretty and unusual receptacles that fasten securely to exterior walls of condominium and cooperative apartments. Annuals can be placed in virtually any container for a season, no matter how frivolous. As long as there are drainage holes, even a ceramic chamber pot or a conch shell will do.

Tulips and pansies in a classically French, square, Versailles-style planter set in front of a trellis, lend a formal appearance to a garden.

Window Gardening

In the summertime, there is nothing lovelier in the city than a town house whose windows are overflowing with colorful blossoms and herbs. Most container requirements such as weather resistance and drainage holes apply to window boxes. Because of hazardous windy conditions, window boxes are prohibited on high-rise buildings. In most cities, having window boxes is against the law. Some permit window boxes only as high up as four to six stories and only if there is no pedestrian traffic underneath. It would be a good idea to check your city's ordinances. Lizzie Boyd's outstanding book *Window Gardens* includes many interesting and innovative ideas for safe, yet attractive, window adornments.

Here is a cross-section of a mix suitable for ground-floor window boxes. A layer of perlite is covered with a layer of charcoal, then several inches of a soil-free mix.

A variety of colors, shapes, and textures grace a box outside this basement window.

Planting Mediums

Topsoil by itself is seldom used in elevated gardens because it is so heavy. Landscape designer Bonnie Billet, of Bonnie Billet Horticulturists, recommends a good, lighter mixture made by combining two parts of topsoil and eight parts of any soil-free mix, which contains peat moss for moisture retention and lightweight mica (instead of sand) for good drainage. Billet's formula calls for lining the bottom of a container with porous fiberglass netting before filling it with her soil-free recipe. This way, you ensure adequate drainage for your plants.

Ken Druse has had good results with a soil-free mix consisting of three parts sphagnum peat moss combined with one part coarse (horticultural-grade) perlite. Perlite is a silica derivative that is only a fraction of the weight of sand. Perhaps the only drawback to a soil-free mix is that it contains no nutrition. But as Druse points out, "The inherent nutrition in topsoil would be depleted after two months in a container. You'll have to add fertilizer in any event. So the lighter-weight medium might be advantageous." Garden centers and nurseries sell prepackaged brands of topsoil and also carry a wide variety of soil-free mixtures.

First discovered in the 1860s, *hydroponics* is a system of gardening in which plants grow aquarium style in an all-nutrient solution that the roots absorb by osmosis. In the United States, it is primarily used as a farming technique for growing vegetables and herbs. The National Aeronautics and Space Administration of the United States is developing hydroponics for its proposed space stations. Although somewhat futuristic, this method could offer exciting possibilities for city gardeners. Israel's abundance of fruits and flowers is largely due to the country's extensive use of hydroponics. Those interested in pursuing hydroponics should consult Richard E. Nicholls's *Hydroponics Soilless Gardening.*

DRIP IRRIGATION SYSTEMS

The one constant need in your city garden is adequate watering. Rain water tends to fall off a plant's leaves, spill over the sides of the container, and never penetrate the planting mix. In our busy, hectic city lives, we can't always count on hand watering. Even if you live and work at home, there is always a chance that you might have to rush out unexpectedly. And if you forget to water the plants, it spells trouble for the garden. For these reasons, installing a drip irrigation system in your container or ground-level garden can make your life easier and, perhaps, save the life of your garden.

Such a device works like the human circulatory system. Like arteries, inconspicuous hoses carry water to the containers. Like capillaries, skinny little "invisible" tubes called hydroinoculators go directly into the soil. Drip irrigation systems work by timers so that every individual container automatically gets watered. The cost of a drip irrigation system varies greatly. Mr.

Van Zelst estimates that it can range from five to thirty percent of the total landscape project's cost, depending on the size of the garden and the system used. However, experienced city gardeners attest to its indispensability.

Elevated city gardens grow better with drip irrigation systems. Without them, soil is more likely to dry out in the summer, and roots are more likely to sustain damage in winter. Because the moisture level in the soil is maintained at the proper level, the survival rate of the garden is increased immeasurably. Additionally, since each container gets only the precise amount of moisture it needs, drip irrigation systems actually conserve water.

For a ground-level garden in a courtyard, a drip irrigation system also saves you time with the garden hose. Installing the system here may be a little more complicated, however, as the pipes must be installed underground, both for aesthetics and to preserve the life of the system.

Before you begin an extensive planting scheme, consult your local nursery and irrigation specialist to be sure your system will suit your needs.

You should be able to locate an irrigation designer-installer in the telephone book, or ask your nursery to recommend someone. An irrigation specialist will service your system and adjust it seasonally, even in periods of water shortage. In late fall, the irrigation specialist turns off and blows air out of the system. This helps create an equilibrium between the amount of moisture in the soil and the amount of moisture in the roots. It also helps reduce one of the leading garden killers—winter root damage. On a smaller, less expensive scale, fine drip-irrigation kits produced by Gardena System of West Germany can be purchased. They are available at larger garden centers, from good gardening-supply sources like Smith & Hawken (catalog), and sometimes at botanical garden shops.

© Derek Fell

This is a close up of one of the hydroinoculators or "capillaries" in a drip-irrigation system. Working on a timer, the indispensable system makes sure everything automatically gets watered.

CHAPTER THREE

ELEMENTS OF DESIGN

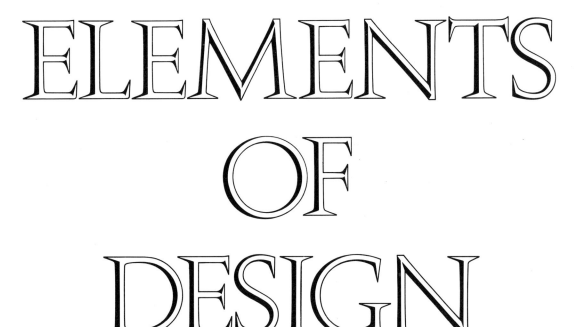

THE VIEW FROM YOUR WINDOW

SCALE, COMPOSITION, AND PERSPECTIVE

COLOR, SHAPE, AND TEXTURE

SURFACES, LAWNS, AND GROUNDCOVERS

DESIGNING FOR YEAR-ROUND INTEREST

LIGHTING AND NIGHT GARDENS

© Ken Druse

*T*he preeminent twentieth-century land-scape architect Thomas D. Church theorized in his well-known work *Gardens Are For People* (McGraw-Hill: New York, 1983), "No definite style of garden from the past answers all the needs of today's small garden.... Even the term garden has changed its meaning.... The new kind of garden is still supposed to be looked at. But that is no longer its only function. It is designed primarily for living. ...How well it provides for the many types of living that can be carried on outdoors is the new standard by which we judge a garden." In other words, once you've determined how you're going to *use* your garden, you can get to work and start designing.

In our heart of hearts, most of us hope to create a dazzling display of horticultural beauty and ornamentation. Even when there is very little elbowroom outside, there is no exultation that compares to showing off your garden to an appreciative audience. When you start thinking about the design of your city garden, allow yourself the freedom to experiment. There are so many suggestions, formulas, and how-tos in garden design that most should only be used as guidelines rather than taken as mandates. Yes, you can recreate what you have admired in the pages of a magazine or in someone else's garden. As in life, however, even if you follow every dictate, there is no guarantee things will turn out exactly as you plan. Most importantly, you must ensure that after the garden has been constructed, its design will contain your own unique imprint. Establish a theme; anchor the design with a pleasing diversity that also incorporates unbroken harmony. By doing so, you

© Alex Roy

Above: *A formal design has been chosen for the garden gracing the front of this brownstone. The window boxes and planters are identical, as are the vines and plant materials in each.*
Below: *Graceful boughs, water, and statuary lend a subtle Oriental influence to this serene, Washington, D.C., town house garden.*

© Ken Druse

will have reaffirmed an affinity with nature.

Space permitting, there is no greater joy than entertaining outside in the warm seasons. A minimum of soft lighting is necessary if you are planning to make the most of your garden at night (see page 52), and if there's room to do so, allow space for seating, an end table, or—if your garden is spacious enough—a small dining or buffet table. Guests, of course, are one thing, but insects are another. Insects are drawn to light, so try to keep lighting subdued.

Some form of shelter from hot sun and sudden showers would be appreciated by friends and family alike. Canvas awnings can be both pretty and practical and are easy to roll up and put away. One family who lives in Zurich, Switzerland, has a beloved old rose pergola. For three generations, at dusk, covered in dense foliage with roses cascading down its sides, it has been a scented summer dining room.

Should you wish only to grow a food garden, you can still make it pretty. There are many ornamental vegetables that are as decorative as they are delicious (see page 67). There are some flowers, like marigolds, which naturally repel pests. They can be grown simultaneously with vegetables. Vegetables welcome some shade in the summertime, so consider planting a fruit tree or two.

However you plan to use your garden, following a few simple design guidelines will save you the headache and expense of replacing plants or features that just don't work. Before you do anything, draw a rough plan of your garden, or consult a professional garden designer, so that the execution of the plan is as spectacular as your original concept.

Cale Roberts' fantastic atrium design of plants, lights, and varying textures is beautiful both day and night.

THE VIEW FROM YOUR WINDOW

© Richard Mandelkorn

Parisians have mastered the art of creating small courtyard gardens that are beautiful when viewed from above. Summer flowers cover the outside walls. An evergreen parterre poised between cobblestones adds interest throughout the year. Looking down at it in winter, its lacy pattern glistens like the frosting on a snowy white cake.

Attention should be directed to some intriguing feature in the distance so that the garden seems to become a part of the magical skyscape. Take advantage of anything interesting or beautiful that lies beyond your garden. Does your apartment face the mountains or rise above a lake or a river? Can you see the Empire State Building or the John Hancock Building? Is the Golden Gate Bridge or the Brooklyn Bridge visible from your terrace? Does your apartment overlook a park or other natural view? If there is a beautiful picture out there, you can "frame" it. Plant tall Italian cypress trees on the left and right of the view. Place dwarf evergreens beside them and "underline" the vista with a low row of evergreen shrubs. If you're fortunate enough to have a view of someone else's beautifully designed garden, try to incorporate this scenery into your garden.

All too often, however, our apartments adjoin garbage-strewn roofs, abut dead-end walls, and confront laundry rooms. (And those are some of the nicer "views.") Undaunted city gardeners cleverly screen out unsightly views with trees, foliage-covered trellises, or rows of tall potted plants. If you have a rooftop, ter-

Opposite: Container plants frame a magnificent Charles River view in Boston. Lightweight, portable furniture is easily brought indoors during bad weather. **Below:** A brightly colored and reliable plant, forsythia can camouflage necessary but unsightly features like this chain-link fence. **Right:** Circular, rhythmically repeated shrubbery effectively softens the narrow outlines of this city garden. Flowering trees planted against the back wall draw the eye into the garden and provide the illusion of spaciousness.

© Alex Roy

race, or penthouse garden, parapet walls often are required by city ordinance to be a permanent construction of no less than 43 inches (1.2 meters) high. Even though walls should enhance or detract from the view as you wish, make certain your parapet walls comply with local regulations. A painted facade of an attractive eighteenth-century English architectural folly or other garden-house structure can be transposed onto wallboard and attached to an opposite wall (with the owner's consent, of course.)

© Derek Fell

SCALE, COMPOSITION, AND PERSPECTIVE

Perhaps no other garden on earth is as symbiotically integrated with architecture as is the city garden. The city's very soul seems expressed in city garden design. Often, form and design follow the urban contour. Like skyscrapers, rooftop and ground-floor city garden designs extend upward. The vertical plane of tree and trellis reflect the city's own expansion heavenward to conserve space. Container plantings and espaliers (trained trees on fences) reflect the city's intent to employ its precious horizontal space advantageously. Yet, the city garden is ultimately an urban refuge, a place to reaffirm our affinity with nature.

Scale, how one part of the design relates to another, is the fundamental design element that makes the plants and objects in your garden a cohesive whole. With proper scale, the relationship and size of each element to the other is proportionate—no part of the garden detracts from another unless you want it to. Scale also concerns how the garden relates to the environment around it and vice versa. One should feel gently compelled to enter the garden and just as pleased to reenter the apartment. Pay close attention to what is placed just outside the entryway to the garden as the transition from inside to outside is as important as what's in your garden. Plants and ornaments at the entryway should serve to introduce one to the garden's composition.

Within the garden, oversize plants may upset the scale of a small garden. Yet, large flowers like peonies can attract attention inward and away from an unattractive view. Too many plants, too many colors, and too many ornaments are distracting and unsettling. Create a rhythm and movement as in a watercolor painting. For relaxation of the senses and easier maintenance, keep things simple.

The arrangement of a container garden depends upon three factors. You have to counterbalance growing conditions, weight restrictions, and available space. Refer to the written plan you've made. Linda Yang, in her excellent book The Terrace Gardener's Handbook—a helpful guide for all city gardeners—suggests that you use chalk to begin marking out spots on the terrace's surface where you're considering placing trees, shrubs, and flowers. This way you'll have a good idea of how all the pieces will work together.

Many landscapers suggest grouping smaller and larger containers together. On

Left: *A translucent glass wall broadens the perspective of this small courtyard by diffusing the boundaries of the space without obstructing available light.* **Right:** *Terra-cotta containers of geraniums dramatically adorn the entrance of a Charleston, South Carolina, town house.*

© Ken Druse

The technique of trompe l'oeil has been used in this garden to suggest that it extends well beyond the brick wall.

a penthouse or large terrace, a wooden platform, or dunnage may have to be erected for them to rest on so that the weight is distributed evenly. Long, thin terraces can be broken up by curvilinear arrangements of planters of multiple heights to disguise the narrowness.

How the backyard city garden is arranged, however, depends entirely on growing conditions and how much space you have. If you're planning to make a raised bed, consider first how large or small it should be in relation to the rest of the garden. Existing trees and shrubs are usually a bonus. Even fallen trees, so long as they are not rotting, can add an unusual acadian influence to the city garden. When ivies and other trailing plants are grown over them, a backyard can be transformed into a sylvan setting.

There may be a tree growing somewhat intrusively right in the middle of your small plot. But before you chop it down, consider pruning away some top growth so shade-loving flowers can grow around it. Or, you could encircle it with a Victorian cast-iron or rustic wooden tree bench.

Perspective in garden design deals with the spatial relationship of objects as they ultimately appear to the eye. This differs from scale in that perspective concerns how elements work together to draw the eye into or around the garden. Trompe l'oeil, for example, is a technique that literally "fools the eye" into believing that a painted wall is actually an extension of the garden. Latticework, painted murals, and sometimes even mirrors are combined to make the garden appear longer or larger. Using perspective, the designer can create optical illusions that create space in a small garden or enclose space in a garden with, for example, an unsightly view.

Another method of suggesting length and space is to make a path from the apartment that gets thinner as it stretches from the doorway. Tall plantings on either side of a small statue or gate at the path's end complete the illusion of depth.

COLOR, SHAPE, AND TEXTURE

An artistic approach to garden *color* resembles that of the nineteenth-century impressionist painters. With a light and subtle blending of colors, you can draw the eye around the garden. Dark objects, such as brown-stained wooden trellises, make the garden recede, while light-colored structures attract attention.

Color variety, however, is somewhat a matter of taste. What is dignified and harmonious to one person can seem boring and lifeless to another. Although many landscape designers advocate limiting color within a narrowly defined range, make a color arrangement that is ultimately going to please you. At first, beginners should limit extensive color experimentation to using fast-blooming annuals; if you're unhappy with the color scheme, something new can be tried the following year.

On the whole, pale colors are the easiest to work with. Soft, creamy whites and ivory are pretty with just about every color, and pale yellows mix nicely with mauve, lilac, and blue. Underplantings of the gray-foliaged Artemisia species and the *Senecio cineraria* (identical to dusty miller) show roses off to great advantage. When using stronger colors, always consider their intensity and the hue. Bright reds, oranges, and very strong flower colors can be used to lead the eye around the composition. Strong purples blend well with delicate mauves and pale lavenders. Scarlet and crimson look good with true white or rosy pink. Many designers advocate using strong colors in the foreground followed by a subtle fading through the spectrum in the center, finally blending to buttery pinks and soft white hues in the background.

Tropical climates offer the most luxuriant palette of brilliant colors. A big, bushy, bold magenta bougainvillea may stand beside canary-yellow allemandas and salmon-colored hibiscus flowers. Part of the magic of these gardens is that nothing

© Sandra Dos Passos

Green euonymus, reddish barberry, and golden daylilies planted below a smooth, white stone wall sculpture exemplify how color, shape, and texture combine in the well-designed garden.

seems to clash. It sometimes appears that the more variety there is in these gardens, the better they look!

However, even in those paradisiacal climates, it isn't color alone that makes the garden beautiful. In every hardiness zone, there are varieties of plants whose leaf colorations, shapes, patterns, forms, and textures can be used decoratively. My favorite variegated leafy plants are green-and-yellow hostas, glossy green-and-white hollies, and splotchy, multicolored crotons. Many gray plants like lamb's ear

are also noteworthy for their felty textures, while others, like yucca leaves, which are long and swordlike, contribute form.

The most prominent features in the garden design are trees and shrubs. Designers use the *shape* of these plants to add decorative effects to the garden. There are many wonderful shapes to work with: horizontal and somewhat rectangular like honey locust; round or flat topped and umbrella shaped like an almond; graceful weeping forms, such as cherries and willows; wedge-shaped or conical varieties

The variety of color, shape, and texture in this small corner of Victor Nelson's garden is lovely.

such as a Bradford pear; fastigiate or vertical trees, which include the majestic ginkgo; and curving and spiraling trees like crab apples, which are particularly lovely forms in the city garden.

Although they require much pruning and take time to be completed, *espaliered,* or trained trees, seem particularly appropriate in city gardens. *The Oxford Companion to Gardens* defines an espalier as "a line of fruit trees whose branches are pruned and trained into formal patterns against a wall or fence, so as to make the most of sunshine and warmth. The wall itself against which they lean can also be called an espalier." A popular use of this technique is an espalier of fruit trees on a very sunny west- or south-facing wall. But you can espalier just about anything: Espaliered camellias are particularly sophisticated, while elegant designs along an open wire or wood fence can be braided, fanned, oblique, or tiered. The Verrier espalier, named for Louis Verrier, a nineteenth-century French gardener, resembles the noble menorah. Espaliers can also be made into geometric forms—diamonds, squares, or wavy lines expressive of art nouveau.

Shadowy areas in a garden suspend uniformity and add *texture* and depth to the composition. Trees are the best natural means of achieving shade in the garden. Trellises, arbors, pergolas, and lath houses are garden structures that can add height and shape as well as shade to a design. They can be built against a wall or, as in roof gardens, placed apart in a carefully chosen position. Made of redwood, cedar, bamboo, and other treated woods or even from fiberglass, such structures can be covered with sweet peas, morning glories, wisteria, pyracantha, moonvine, and any other vine or climbing plant.

Another technique of creating shade on exposed roofs is to plant a row of hedges to cast afternoon shade. This can provide limited morning or afternoon shade for plants, such as variegated dogwood and coleus, which are less tolerant of full, all-day sunshine.

SURFACES, LAWNS, AND GROUNDCOVERS

Slate, tile, brick, stone, and wood surfacing should harmonize with a garden's planting scheme. Surfacing can play a particularly important part in covered porches. Exquisitely tiled, a floor can become a focal point in itself.

Surfaces of washed pebbles and pea gravel are recommended by many city garden designers. On small high-rise balconies, weight restrictions prohibit adding any surfacing other than what is already there. If you decide to add tile or slate to your penthouse, in most places the law dictates that the material cannot be thicker than 1 inch (2.5 centimeters). The roof should be prepared properly to avoid leakage problems later on. Mr. Van Zelst

says, "To prepare a roof properly, copper flashing all around the perimeter is necessary. If it already exists, check for holes. Old seams should be resoldered. Roof surfaces should be primed and then layered with hot tar, tar paper, and fiberglass netting. A reputable roofing company will be acquainted with these practices. Ask for a minimum of a fifteen-year guarantee."

Wooden decks are best constructed of a number of small-sized pieces of lumber for access to a roof's surface. Each plank should be light enough to be lifted by one or two people. The construction should allow for expansion of the wood. Durable woods such as redwood and cedar are

Above left: *The curving redwood deck of this San Francisco garden helps unify the design and complements a plum tree's coppery leaves in the background.*

Above right: *Tile, wood, and a dense groundcover of English ivy blend to create this roof garden by Halstead Welles.*

often used as they are most resistant to the effects of weathering. But a good carpenter can suggest just the right wood for your location.

An uneven backyard surface can be regraded, but a slope may require a raised platform. Slate can be applied to a foundation of either concrete or sand, and tiles can be used only with a concrete foundation. Bricks and cobblestones, on the other hand, require a sand base. When drainage is poor, surfaces tend to deteriorate, and a drainage pipe should be placed underneath beforehand.

Backyard walkways can be constructed of slate or flagstone in rectangular, oval, or naturally formed shapes. Particularly attractive walkways are those that are constructed of natural flagstones with moss, clover, periwinkle, or fragrant thyme protruding from the spaces in between. If there's enough direct sunlight for three hours a day, and if you have enough space for one, you might want to consider a lawn. Everything you've heard about them is true. They can be difficult to grow

and maintain, but it's such a thrill to have your own little plot of green grass just outside the back door. For small city greenswards, it is best and easiest to use purchased sod. You'll need a planed-off surface with 6 inches (15 centimeters) of topsoil to put on it. Underneath the topsoil, if necessary, place a 3-inch (7.5-centimeter) diameter drainage pipe in 3 inches of gravel.

In most sheltered gardens, however, too much shade makes growing a lawn impossible. Although many cannot be walked on, there are several groundcovers that make pretty substitutes. An excellent source for suggestions is Ortho Books's *All About Ground Covers*.

Astroturf™ is an option for those too-shady areas, but you'll be better off with the more attractive, natural groundcovers. Astroturf is impractical as it does not dry, and, as a result, it grows a fungus that can grow unprotected and turn the *faux* turf black within two years. Stay away from this artificial cover unless you are prepared to replace it after it rots.

English ivies are particularly pretty when located near city brick walls. This variety is called Hedera helix *'Erecta'*.

Above left: *Pots of bushy orange lantana on a flagstone terrace create a visual transition into a grassy lawn, the most prized of all ground covers. Designed by Oehme, van Sweden & Associates.* **Above right:** *The groundcover between city row houses can be attractively paved with flagstones.*

DESIGNING FOR YEAR-ROUND INTEREST

Many gardeners become bored and restless with what seems to be the never-ending green of midsummer. In small-space gardens, one should avoid planting flowers whose blooms will fade very quickly. Lovely as they are, lilacs, cabbage, and moss roses bloom for a very short time. Actually, there is no reason, other than poor planning, why there cannot be something flowering from early spring to late fall. Look at nature's own growing cycle: white snowdrops, pussy willows, pale yellow-green weeping willows, bright yellow forsythia, brilliant pink and red tulips, vibrant green grass, and violet-blue Jacob's ladder of spring. Melon-toned daylilies, multicolored zinnias, and a host of other annuals carry the color through the summer. Quietly colorful chrysanthemums and luminescent dahlias give way to fall's blazing red, orange, and gold, eventually fading into the rich and varied browns and grays of winter. Carefully choose your plants for their shape, color, fragrance, and timing.

When the flowers are gone and the last autumn leaves are strewn about the garden, there can be something to look forward to if you have planted for year-round interest. Autumn- and winter-flowering witch hazels (Hamamelis spp.) are cherished by many city gardeners. Some trees are covered in magnificently colored and patterned barks. Silvery birches and aspen, the Zelkova (Zelkova sinica), mottled in a plethora of green shades, white-and-gray snow gum (Eucalyptus niphophila), and foamy green and pink-brown lacebark pine (Pinus bungeana) are a few examples. The bark of the evergreen P. nigra looks like an opaque, brown, stained-glass window.

There are shrubs with colorful twigs in winter, such as red-twig dogwood. The leaves of andromeda (Andromeda glaucophylla) turn purple in winter, as do some species of juniper. The leaves of evergreens of the genus Arctostaphylus turn bronze in winter. Heaths and heathers will also add color to the winter landscape. Many holly plants (Ilex spp.) bear red and yellow berries in fall and winter.

A beautifully shaped tree is a lovely living sculpture. Some especially graceful bare winter trees are magnolias, crape myrtles, and willows. Among willows, Salix matsudana is recommended for its evocative, twisting shape. Like beautifully shaped bare trees and evergreens, statuary and weatherproofed ornaments add interest to a garden's design throughout the year. Looking out the window on a bleak winter night, when dramatic lighting emphasizes tree shapes, evergreens, and ornamentation, the garden will be as interesting and attractive as it is in summer.

© Sandra Dos Passos

Left: Marigolds, coleus, and other annuals can only be grown in the spring and summer. **Opposite page, above left:** Trees and shrubs with bare branches look especially beautiful coated with ice or sparkling snow. **Above right:** Anemones and tulips are just a few of spring's dazzling array. **Below right:** Autumn's blazing leaf colors can be enjoyed just as easily in the city. **Below left:** Lush vines are a sure sign of summer's presence in the city.

LIGHTING AND NIGHT GARDENS

Looking up at a clear, moonlit night sky through the bare branches of a tree, it is easy to visualize what Van Gogh painted on some of his canvases. But even when there is a full moon, does it bathe your garden in its special light? Artificial lighting can complement the soothing, tranquil nature of the nightscape and be a gentle guide to explore the mysteries of a different dimension—the night garden. Lighting shouldn't compete with the glittering city skyline, but rather, be a gracious, if not exciting, extension of it. Lighting may not be as important to your garden as it is to more decorative ones, but some outdoor lighting would make it possible for you to do garden work at night, to entertain in the garden, or to simply enjoy looking at it.

Subtlety is the key to effective lighting. You want to see what is being lit without the source of the light being visible. One has, in essence, the ability to recreate an entirely new garden out of the darkness. There are many features that are not always visible during the day, and these can be played up to full advantage at night. Night lighting is best used to create and accentuate garden aspects such as the shadow of a beautiful tree, a curious configuration of twigs, a tiny statue, or a neoclassical pillar overflowing with sparkling white clematis. The right lighting can turn a weeping willow into a shimmering fountain of light. Arbors and other garden structures are strong features to highlight. Additionally, illuminating gargoyles, chimneys, eaves, gables, dormer windows, columns, and architectural features like decorative friezes, capitals, and tympanums on neighboring buildings can add a spectacular dimension to the night garden. Just as you can use light to bring out shape and form, you can use darkness to block out what you don't want to see.

Electric wiring should be concealed for aesthetics as well as safety, and it must be impervious to water. There are lighting kits available, but do not compromise quality

Lit from below, this bosk of little-leaf linden trees in the Hamilton Garden of Columbus, Indiana, is very alluring. Even in daylight, the silhouettes of the tree branches stand out like living sculptures. Designed by Dan Kiley.

© Balthazar Korab/Design: Dan Kiley Landscape Architecture

for cost. Gardeners are cautioned not to attempt installation without professional advice—an electrician is mandatory. Electricians, however, are not designers. It is better to consult a professional landscape-illumination specialist to achieve the results you want.

Lighting systems can be manually or automatically controlled by timers or photocells, which are solar-powered devices that turn lights on at dusk, off at daybreak. There are also some computer software programs being developed for automatic operation of garden lighting. Remote-control switches can be conveniently located inside the apartment so you can enjoy night views from inside, and dimmers offer flexibility.

Tiny, low-voltage lights very often are used to illuminate trees. Landscape-lighting designers prefer incandescent white light. These masters of illumination have innumerable filters for capturing the romance of the night garden. While one filter attempts to duplicate the color of moonlight, another can create flesh-flattering tones for down-lighting a dining table.

Other popular garden lighting fixtures include Japanese lanterns, the Mexican tin *lampion* with pinpoint holes for light filtration, and antique and other lighting fixtures, which can be mounted on the outside wall of your apartment. For the sole enjoyment of them after night falls, landscape architect Charlotte Frieze of New York City suggests adding plants with iridescent and evening-fragrant flowers. Dogwoods, birches, white-flowered periwinkles, lilies, impatiens, caladiums, azaleas, and rhododendrons show up well at night. I recommend the exotic smell of night-blooming jasmine, night-blooming cactus, creeping rosemary, or evening primrose. There are some fragrant, night-blooming orchids that grow in tropical gardens. Other flowers with heavenly scents include nicotiana, petunias, stephanotis, wisteria, freesia, hyacinth, and many other trumpet-shaped flowers.

The Lure of Fragrance

And because the breath of flowers is far sweeter in the air (where it comes and goes like the warbling of music) than in the hand, therefore nothing is more fit for that delight, than to know what be the flowers and plants that do best perfume the air.

—Francis Bacon, *Of Gardens*

*B*y all means, locate a few fragrant plants near seating areas to enhance the appeal of your garden. Like most herbs, many plants have aromatic leaves. Use this list to select the most fragrant plants.

Common Name	Latin Name	Description
Angel's Trumpet*	*Datura* spp.	Heavy musk
Bachelor's button	*Centaurea imperialis*	Light and airy
Carnation	*Dianthus* spp.	
Creeping Rosemary*	*Rosmarinus officinalis*	Herbaceous
Freesia*	*Freesia x Kewensis*	Delicate
Gardenia	*Gardenia jasminoide*	Sweet and heavy
Geranium (scented)*	*Pelargonium*	Lemon or rose
Globe thistle*	*Eclrinops exaltatus*	
Hyacinth	*Muscari* bulbs	
Jasmine	*Jasminium* spp.	Springtime perfume
Lavender	*Lavandula* spp.	Sweet and heavy
Orange and lemon trees	*Citrus* spp.	
Pot Marigold	*Calendula*	Earthy
Rose*	*Rose* varieties	
Stephanotis	*Stephanotis floribunda*	Fresh and flowery
True Sweet Bay Laurel	*Laurus nobilis*	Herbaceous
Wisteria	*Wisteria sinensis*	Light and sweet

*Use for fragrance at night

Grape Hyacinth   Bachelor's Button

CHAPTER FOUR

CITY STYLES

FORMAL

INFORMAL

MINIMALIST

ORIENTAL

SHADE GARDENS

FRUIT AND VEGETABLE GARDENS

SCULPTURE GARDENS

COMMUNITY GARDENS

© Ken Druse

In the classic book *The Principles of Gardening* (Simon & Schuster: New York, 1984), Hugh Johnson equates straight edges and architecture with formal gardens and flowing and naturalistic forms with informal gardens. He writes that "modern . . . and small gardens frequently have no straight lines or traditional formality, yet their flowing forms are definitely not of nature's making. Their spiritual ancestors are the works of Mondrian, Picasso or [Henry] Moore."

Johnson recognizes that a garden's style takes its cues from painting and sculpture and emphasizes the need for the design to take these artistic techniques into account in a garden's plan. Therefore, a garden's style can reflect the artistic tenets of a particular era or culture. Additionally, Johnson's comparison of a garden to architecture is particularly applicable to the city garden. Because your garden is located amid buildings, it is appropriate for you to relate its style to that of its surroundings. You can also choose to juxtapose the garden's style with the look of the city, further highlighting its unique qualities.

Whether you are starting from scratch in the backyard or working with an old, or neglected garden, begin thinking about your garden in one of two ways: as a means of recreating the outdoor landscape of a bygone era or as something completely new. If your site is new, you might want to model your garden on historic gardens in the area. If you are adapting an existing garden, consider what residents may have done with the space before. Some roof and terrace gardens, for example, have existed since the 1920s. However, the weight of masonry construction, soil, and water damage are forcing these lovely old gardens, one by one, out of existence. Because of more stringent building codes and ordinances, owners are being compelled to grow plants only in containers.

If you happen to be one of these romantic souls who prefers the lovely antique appearance of a rooftop garden, but is being forced to comply to building codes

Courtesy Morgan Wheelock Inc. Landscape Architects

This is an outstanding example of dignified city terrace design that relates the garden to its surroudings. The superimposed balustrade acts on a nexus; the eye is then led outward to the city's architecture.

In this outdoor space, a variety of structural forms and gravel surfaces establish the modern design scheme. Evocative neon lighting is an exciting and appropriate alternative to traditional lamps.

A nineteenth century limestone bust, a period bench, brick, marble, and terra-cotta surfaces, and a profusion of cascading ivy, tulips, daisies, foxgloves, and hyacinths lend an old-fashioned richness to this restored period garden.

(see page 22), there is good news. At a symposium on landscape architecture trends in 1987, Diane Kostial McGuire, renowned landscape architect and garden adviser to Dumbarton Oaks in Washington, D.C., said, "One doesn't have to wipe the blackboard clean—the garden isn't just one more place where our culture and heritage have to be sacrificed." Fortunately, there is now a great surge in preserving the appearance of these old city gardens.

Those converting their old penthouses to container gardens might easily be able to conserve the original design by duplicating the masonry or brick in fiberglass façades and attaching them to new, wooden containers. Weatherproof, simulated brick and mortar wallboard can be erected (with weep holes for drainage) to resemble the original masonry walls, behind which new containers can be placed.

If you have a ground-level garden and live near a landmark or in an area of historic preservation, you might also want to consider a period restoration design. If alterations have been made to the original home site over the centuries, you may even wish to recreate a period garden that previous occupants might have enjoyed. Botanical garden libraries and historical societies can be good sources from which to learn more about garden history.

If you want or need a completely new garden, however, chances are you'll have to develop slowly from old to new. Starting entirely from scratch can be prohibitively expensive—combine the old containers with the new to get started. Over time, you can do away with the elements of the garden that don't suit you.

For best results, I recommend contacting a landscape architect. You can find one through the local chapter of the Society of Landscape Architects. In conjunction with a landscape professional, you can create a container garden using lightweight soil mixtures and containers with façades resembling the old, heavy masonry. In this way, historical flavor can be preserved.

FORMAL

Perhaps the truest forerunner of today's formal urban garden is the walled Persian *pardes*, or paradise garden. In the scorching heat, a highly controlled, rectangular space was created, which was crisscrossed with four water courses that met in the center. The entire space was walled in. Within the confines of these very elegant gardens, royalty lounged in the soothing shade of porticoes and surrounding trees.

In the Italian Renaissance villa landscape tradition, the connection between architecture and garden was integral and apparent. The garden's contours followed the geometric lines of the architecture. Viewed from any angle, a garden's symmetrical visual field dominated the composition. At Versailles, the French extended and expanded on the concept by transforming a great expanse of land into a masterfully planned garden that exemplifies the extent to which nature can be artfully manipulated.

Even in the modern urban garden, the tenets of formality—geometry, order, structure, and control—are evident. In admiring such well-executed designs, one senses the presence of the clarity, logic, and philosophy of Rene Descartes, mathematician and cofounder of analytical geometry. Borders of boxwood and yew, clipped hedges, trained plants, and topiary— the epitome of control — are common in the formal garden. Sleek, elegant, or period-inspired furniture and ornamentation complement the design.

In introducing symmetry to create a formal garden, you will have to arrange all garden elements so that they are proportionately situated. For example, if you have a clipped hedge of Korean box, a nearby bench must be placed parallel to the hedge. Additionally, the bench should be perfectly centered along the length of the hedge. Paths must be perfectly straight and should be constructed of uniformly spaced and shaped paving materials.

Sculptural and other decorative features must also conform to the basic formal plan. For example, if there is a sculpture of Venus to the right of the path, there should be one of Adonis situated equidistant from the path to the left. If there are three ornate terra-cotta planters, each should be identical and they should be geometrically aligned; if they are arranged in a straight line, they should be evenly spaced. Each planter should contain the same color combinations and be of the same design. For instance, each planter could contain pink verbenas growing in the center, edged by red verbenas.

Formal designs also demand that flowers be planted in rows or neatly defined areas. The beds are rigorously, geometrically patterned. Begonias, salvias, geraniums, ageratum, zinnias, chrysanthemums, and dusty miller are commonly used, because they provide a reliable block of color that continues to bloom all season long. Borders should be clipped and contoured to contribute to the overall symmetry. For instance, if you plant a bed of tall pink begonias on one side of a path, there should be an identically colored bed of begonias of the same height on the other side of the path.

During the process of planning a formal garden, always think in terms of harmonic proportions. If you feel you need more tangible inspiration, you could visit an exemplary formal garden in your region. Your local horticultural society or botanical garden library can provide you with more information.

© Sandra Dos Passos

The lines throughout this small formal garden located in Savannah, Georgia, follow the rectangular, architectural shape. Beds are uniformly shaped and evenly spaced apart.

INFORMAL

The eighteenth-century philosopher and writer Jean Jacques Rousseau believed that the human being and the garden alike should be allowed to develop free of limiting intervention. Building on the momentum of such a philosophy, the romantic period of the nineteenth century was attracted to and fueled by a deep reverence for the informal, untamed beauty of nature. Ironically, however, it was in a London garden and not in the pastoral English countryside that John Keats wrote his famous "Ode to a Nightingale."

During the eighteenth and early nineteenth centuries in Europe, people came to believe that garden formality itself should be restrained. Plants were allowed to grow out. There was a new feeling for natural meandering and undulating forms. The popularity of this style has given rise to a variety of informal designs from the rustic style populated with simple yet appealing wooden furniture to the wild garden, a self-sustaining native-plant environment first proposed by William Robinson in 1870 in his book *The Wild Garden*.

The asymmetry of an informal garden is the essence of its design. "Your planning should expose the inherent forms of nature," says garden writer Edwin T. Morris. The purpose is to expose and highlight the natural growth patterns of plants. Therefore, the informal urban garden takes on a more free-form look and allows nature to create an ever-changing array of shapes. Patterns are more organic than the square, triangle, or rectangle forms found in the formal garden, and the natural shapes of plants create spatial, and even symbolic, relationships. For example, a clump of silvery artemesia resembling the shape of a drop of water can create natural garden symbolism. Despite the free use of shapes, colors, and textures, even an informal garden has to be planned. Unlike a formal garden, however, the plan is harder to detect. The gardener must draw up a planting plan to achieve a pleasing variety

© Ken Druse

Victor Nelson's informal Manhattan roof garden has been entirely created from a clever arrangement of containers. One contains a willow, a dogwood, and a birch tree. Others feature azaleas, lilies, hostas, violets, and ferns.

of textures, heights, and shapes. You may have apricot roses growing in front of a wall of ivy with creamy foxgloves, shell-pink phlox, and silvery, fernlike *centaurea gymnocarpa* in the foreground.

To begin planning, decide where plants should be raised and where they should be left at ground level. Colors should be artfully blended with one another. Warm colors should be kept together. A good warm-color balance, for instance, is a container of red and magenta geraniums combined with orange-red zinnias and coralbells. Similarly, cool colors should be combined. Clematis, hollyhocks, lavender, and delphiniums blend for a cool blue look. Gardens landscaped with flowers of only one color say, white, are considered informal. But it takes a lot of skill to effectively achieve this look.

Wild gardens are informal, but their plants are selected for interesting shapes, colors, and contours. A mix of plant types is emphasized, and subtle masses of color are encouraged. The wild-garden plan involves using native plants because they are well suited to a region's climate and require less cultivation. In this environment, plants' shapes and hues interact to create subtly beautiful vignettes. In general, the wild garden is a more relaxed outdoor space that brings a spot of nature into the urban setting.

In informal schemes, paths undulate and plantings such as Virginia creeper or ivy trail casually across paths. Oak chips or varying types of fieldstones can create pathways. The furniture and ornamentation in informal gardens shouldn't interfere with the plantings or natural elements and should blend in as much as possible. Trees, rather than elaborate structures, are used for shade.

Furnishings can range from the intentionally rustic to simple and unpretentious selections, which are placed in naturally occurring hollows or where a weeping tree arches. Ornamentation is kept to a minimum. You might decoratively display large natural rocks to show their grain, striation, or naturally occurring crystalline forms, such as quartz or calcite. Birdfeeders and sundials—garden accessories that relate directly to nature—are also appropriate ornaments for the informal garden. Ornamentation can also include tree stumps fringed with delicately colored lichen, fungi, and mushrooms. There are several that resemble underwater algae, sea coral, and lacy aquatic plants. Some exquisite examples include the aptly named coral fungus (*Clavicorona pyxidata*) and the speckled, rubbery Dryad's saddle, (*Polyporus squamosus*).

Beds and containers should be filled (but not overcrowded) with shrubs and perennials and underplanted with groundcovers. By adhering to a relaxed garden plan that incorporates a few rustic touches, it is possible to capture the feeling of being out in the country.

This lush rooftop wild garden features purple loose strife and perky black-eyed Susans.

© Ken Druse

MINIMALIST

© Kate Zari 1987

© Allen Carter/Luis Barragan, Architect

A single palm tree leaps out as the only natural element, when featured against blocks of primary colors.

Perfectly embodying the principles of minimalist garden design, this Mondrian-esque garden uses plantings as a focal point, juxtaposes diverse textures, and delineates crisp lines.

The roots of minimalist landscaping probably extend as far back as Stonehenge. However, the contemporary applications of minimalist landscape design grew out of the 1960s minimalist movement in painting and sculpture. Evocative of the later works of Mondrian, minimalist design stresses line, shape, color, and contrast.

Expressed in stone and tile, a minimalist garden is like architecture without a ceiling. With the emphasis on the use of walls and water, planting is restricted in deference to the visual importance of the sharp architectural line of a brightly colored wall. Water is used for its mirroring quality. A long trough, for example, can be used to reflect surrounding buildings or moving clouds. The overall effect is one of conscious serenity. Luis Barragan, architect and minimalist garden designer, says, "In my fountains, silence sings."

The manipulation of space through color and form is also an objective of the minimalist garden. Walls are painted vibrant coral, purple, pink, and lemon hues, which interact to enlarge and shrink space in interesting ways. Sculpturally formed plants like trees with twisted trunks, cacti, and spears of agaves and phormiums can be silhouetted against walls to create contrasts of color and shape.

Interpreting Barragan's ideas for city gardens, landscape architect Charlotte Frieze says, "In a small space you can have a great deal of interest without having too many elements in that space. There is usually just one focal point in the garden, perhaps a trickling fountain. A solitary cherry tree or Japanese maple against a plain background is fabulous. Dense groundcovers such as pachysandra and myrtle can be grown in masses. And the way edges of the stone pavement and the plant material meet is important." Texture can be introduced by mixing differing clumps or tufts of ornamental grasses. For instance, you could mix buff-colored cloud grass (*Agrostis nebulosa*) with green-flowering pearl grass, (*Briza maxima*). Shimmering feather grass (*Stipa pennata*) makes a nice contrast with richly structured, dark lavender statice (*Limonium spp.*).

ORIENTAL

A practical and aesthetic solution to the limited space of city gardens is to create an Oriental-inspired design. Chinese and Japanese garden arts imbue each element with symbolic association. Therefore, even a small space can have great significance and beauty. Says landscape architect Charlotte Frieze, "These gardens are very spiritual. They are meant to offer an experience of transcending everyday life." Oriental gardens were admired by Western visitors and then copied in Europe and North America. One such example is the Japanese garden in Golden Gate Park in San Francisco. And small Japanese gardens began to be added to big estate gardens in the early twentieth century such as those built in Newport, Rhode Island.

Oriental gardens are meant to be sanctuaries of nature, associated with old, refined ways of life and traditions, such as those practiced by Chinese rulers and Buddhist monks. According to Edwin T. Morris, who leads yearly garden tours to China and is the author of *The Gardens of China: History, Art and Meanings,* "Walking into an Oriental garden should be like walking into an Oriental painting. They avoid symmetry, as should the garden designer."

Each of the four seasons is meant to be represented in the Oriental garden. This results in extensive use of evergreens and rocks so that there is year-round color. The garden is used almost like an outdoor room, where such events in nature as moonrises and the blossoming of flowers can be observed and contemplated.

Familiar elements of Oriental garden design are evergreens, azaleas, pines, and rocks and gravel. If space permits, a stone lantern and a pool of goldfish can also be included.

Japanese

A woman once asked a Japanese gardener what gardening meant to him. He smiled and held up his pruning shears! Contrary to what many believe, a Japanese garden can require high maintenance. Such gardens are not formal in the geometric sense, but everything is pruned and very tightly controlled. Although highly contrived, the relative positioning of elements reflects their natural counterparts. For example, in a dry rock garden, rocks, gravel, and sand are positioned to mirror the proportions of a water-bordered landscape.

In addition to each component in the garden having symbolic value—as a mirror of an element in nature—there are four different kinds of garden styles: the dry rock garden, the literary men's garden, the water garden, and the tea garden. The dry rock garden is designed for meditation and the only plants used are mosses. The literary men's garden is generally small and is planned for quiet thought. In the water garden, rocks and plants are placed to lead the viewer through a progression around and over the water. The tea garden serves as an entrance path for the tea ceremony.

Traditionally, paths in Japanese gardens are fraught with significance and are used in all arrangements. In the days when Japan was divided up by feuding warlords and their samurai, the garden path leading up to the teahouse was called "the dewy path." Made of carefully chosen

© Kate Bader

If designed for meditation, Japanese dry rock gardens require only gravel, rock arrangements, and mosses.

rocks and stones and sprinkled with water, the path was said to cause all who walked on it to forget the animosity of the times by concentrating on the dewiness of the approach to the teahouse. The path represents the virtues of restraint, politeness, sensibility, and modesty. Weapons, were mandatorily left at the garden's entrance, and no political conversations were allowed in the garden or teahouse. A squat granite lantern usually lit the path.

Other common elements are fine, smooth-edged white gravel, broken shells, or river stone used among the plantings. They can be laid in a curving manner to highlight plant material. If the element of water is missing, rocks are sometimes arranged to imitate a meandering river bed of dry stone, or the gravel combed to suggest ripples of water. Randomly imbedded granite rocks symbolize a feeling of depth and strength held in reserve.

A predominance of green plants are used in Japanese gardens because color variations are kept to a minimum. Even the much-used azalea is pruned to appear marbleized. Dwarf pines, junipers, conifers, and smaller bamboos suit the Japanese-style city garden perfectly. Groundcovers include grass and mosses, which the Japanese like to use because of their rich coloration and patina. Flowering plants are used sparingly. Those most often chosen are chrysanthemums, gardenias, and water lilies. Although they must fit the scale of your particular site, flowering cherry, plum, peach, and crab-apple trees, whose spreading boughs remain green throughout most of the year, are appropriate in Japanese designs.

© Ken Druse

Water lilies are often planted in Japanese gardens. If you do not have room for a pool, try growing water lilies that are hardy to your area in insulated half-whiskey barrels.

Chinese

Chinese gardening style is relatively rare in North American cities, which is unfortunate. Such gardens are easier to maintain than Japanese gardens, and in many ways suit the city life-style better. Though similar to Japanese gardens in that both glorify nature, the Chinese prefer more color, both in plant materials and furnishings. Plantings are looser and allowed to grow out more freely. The irregular form of the azalea shrub is considered interesting, and the plant is allowed to grow freely, unlike in Japanese gardens.

The composition of Chinese designs is asymmetrical. One often sees pairs of high and low trees or big and small stones situated together, reflecting the design principle of the "guest-host" relationship. Paths are often paved with river stones, which, according to the Chinese, should look as if a bolt of brocade has been unraveled across the garden. An "ocean" of terra-cotta paving or tiling is also used as a hard surface so that is swirls around rock and plant materials.

Typically, seating is a sturdy, hollow, barrellike ceramic. Ming blue, turquoise, canary yellow, and Chinese red are the preferred colors, which are then glazed for a luminous finish. Four holes on top of the seat allow puddles to drain off the surface after a rain shower.

Symbolism in Chinese gardens is manifested in the use of rocks to evoke the nine sacred peaks of China. Groups of rocks

Opposite left: A carefully positioned rock becomes the focal point of a Chinese garden scheme. Trees frame this irregularly shaped feature. ***Opposite right:*** *In a variation on* penjing, *a ceramic container holds a vignette representing towering mountain peaks surrounded by trees.*

Right: The understated quality of Oriental schemes is exemplified by this richly textured paving. A variety of shapes and sizes of stones are interlocked on both horizontal and vertical axes. ***Far right:*** *An "ocean" of complexly patterned paving, an evocative tree, and a simple bench create a meditative setting.* ***Below:*** *An evergreen loquat tree is the perfect ornamental touch in a Chinese design.*

are often placed together and used to evoke a hilly and mountainous landscape. Sometimes a "landscape" of jutting rocks is set on a marble tray. Such a composition is called a *penjing*. Additionally, tiny sprigs or dwarf pine seedlings might be stuck into rock crevices on the tray. Circular lattice-work and rounded ornamental grilles can be used in Chinese city garden design to create the classic moongate.

Aside from their beauty, plants are valued for their symbolism in Chinese gardens. Bamboo, for example, represents resiliency. There are many very hardy bamboos. Two that are grown successfully in cities are golden bamboo *(Phylostachys aurea)* and hard-running bamboo *(Phylostachys nuda)*. Additionally, peach tree flowers, which bloom on naked wood in early spring before the leaves appear, are a symbol of rebirth. Chrysanthemums evoke a Mandarin poet, Tao Yuan-ming, who chose to leave a civil service position to live close to nature. He had to survive in adversity just as chrysanthemums have to bloom in cool weather. Perhaps the most beloved of all flowers is the lotus, which is the embodiment of purity. An eleventh-century poem states that the lotus "rises from foul mud and is not defiled."

Appropriate trees for a Chinese city garden are dwarf pines, juniper cypress, small willows, magnolias, and winter-sweet *(Chimonanthus praecox)*, which smells like jasmine and blooms in late winter or early spring. The Chinese also love fruit trees. Choices include plum (their national flower), evergreen loquat, litchi *(Nephelium litchi)*, orange, peach, and brilliant, red-berried pomegranate trees. Among flowers and shrubs, rosy azaleas, rhododendrons, gardenias, carnations, narcissus, camellias, forsythia, daphne, lilacs, crape myrtle, and the climbing rose *(Rosa banksiae)* are used in profusion. Other popular flowers are peonies, daylilies, irises, morning glories, poppies, dwarf water lilies, and China asters.

SHADE GARDENS

This shady garden incorporates diverse elements including cherry blossoms, yellow flowering broom, and basket of gold. Sun and shade patterns were studied to ensure that each plant receives an appropriate amount of light.

Strangely enough, shady city backyards are sometimes more bosklike than their sunny suburban counterparts. A lack of sunlight doesn't necessarily prevent plants from flourishing. Look at the underbrush in the Amazon!

Designing a shade garden depends on what sort of trees or obstacles are creating the shadow. During spring and summer, scrutinize the overshadowing to determine how the amount of sunlight differs during the day and how it shifts from spot to spot. Some shade-loving plants require more light than others do, and your design will need to conform to the patterns of filtered light and dense shading to accommodate the plants you want to grow. Moreover, you might notice dry, shady conditions on a windswept roof but damp shade in the backyard. While some sites have enough sunlight to grow flowers and ground-covers, other sites are so dark that little more than ferns and decorative mosses will grow.

After assessing conditions, plantings should be selected to suit the mood of the location, which is influenced by the tracery of tree branches and the shape and height of the tree canopy. So much has been written lately on shade plantings that your best bet is to look in the local botanical garden and horticultural society book shops for any publications written about suggested shade plantings specifically for your region.

Plants that thrive in damp, shady conditions are ferns, mosses, blue or white gentians, primroses, marsh marigolds, camellias, and hydrangea quercifolia. For dry, shady conditions, try euphorbias, the foam flower (*Tiarella cordifolia*), foxgloves, the aucuba (*Aucuba japonica*), butchers broom, and pachysandra. Vincas and hostas are good choices for both situations.

FRUIT AND VEGETABLE GARDENS

Space is so tight in city gardens that if you're seriously interested in growing a large variety of vegetables, your best bet is to join an urban community vegetable garden (see page 69). It's also a great way to learn. However, there's no reason you can't create a pretty little snippet of fruits and vegetables on a roof or sunny south-facing terrace.

Increasingly, fruits and vegetables are being bred especially for small-scale gardens. The Bushstar hybrid is a small variety of cantaloupe, while Burpee offers a Missouri midget. There are also many dwarf fruit trees. Among vegetables, cute dwarf carrots (with feathery tops that look like Queen Anne's lace) and cherry tomatoes are very suitable for the urban produce plot.

You probably have more vertical than horizontal space for growing vegetables and fruits. Walls, fences, arbors, poles, and pergolas can be covered with peas, string beans, lima beans, cucumbers, and grapes. Strawberries and raspberries are popular city growers. Sunflowers, corn, red rhubarb, tomatoes, and asparagus are some taller candidates that can do double duty to shade less light-tolerant herbs, flowers, and vegetables growing beneath them.

With excellent results, Cindy Olson, a veteran city vegetable grower, horticulturist, and owner of C.O.R.E. Landscape Contracting, has been disobeying the old rule of planting rows a foot (30.48 centimeters) or more apart. She is able to grow food plants closely together, because her site has very good air circulation. But, Ms. Olson admits that she is very attentive. She constantly inspects for pests or any signs of disease and regularly sprays the undersides of leaves and cleans debris away. "A nice, healthy garden will attract fewer pests and diseases. Be observant!" she advises. One sure way to avoid overcrowding is by planting only a few seedlings. If you are starting from seed, plant no more than half a dozen of them. Or, plant half the packet and thin out weaker plants as they begin to sprout. Ms. Olson has grown zucchini and violets, curly parsley, basil, upright onions, lettuces, tomatoes, nasturtiums, glorious red cabbages, and a companion planting of marigolds (to ward off pests) all in the same small lot.

An efficient approach in small city spaces is to add vegetables for their decorative as well as edible attributes. Most leafy vegetables are beautifully shaped and colored. Many edible flowers and plants are quite lovely. Among the prettiest are pea, bean, okra, and squash blossoms. Some have very lovely fragrances. Spark the design with brightly colored chili, cherry, and bell peppers.

Children can have a lot of fun growing vegetables with you. They enjoy planting things and watching them come up soon afterward; having their own small garden gives them a special feeling of pride when it does produce. Cucumbers, lettuces, beans, and herbs grow very quickly. Test your fruits and vegetables for ripeness as you would in a produce market. They should smell ripe and be firm but not hard. Ms. Olson recommends twisting off, rather than wrenching or pulling, fruits and vegetables from the top of the stem. She uses scissors or pinches off fresh herbs between her thumb and forefinger. *The Beautiful Food Garden: Encyclopedia of Attractive Food Plants* by Kate Rogers Gessert, suggests landscape uses for food plants.

Fruit trees grow very well in containers. You can grow a fruit tree that isn't hardy in your area by leaving it outside only in the summer. To keep it thriving all year, however, you should position it at a window exposure that allows for exactly as much light as the plant needs.

SCULPTURE GARDENS

Above left: *In a Georgetown, Washington, D.C., garden, a Chagall is framed in lush greenery and contrasted with a gravel-covered seating area.*
Above right: *Highlighted by a backdrop of single-form red oleanders, Max Ernst's* In the Streets of Athens *decorates Peggy Guggenheim's sculpture garden in Venice, Italy.*

Early seventeenth-century gardens in Holland consisted mainly of stonework, sculpture, and urns, with perhaps a single tree for greenery. Having flowers in the garden was even frowned upon. Later on, of course, the Dutch fell in love with flowering bulbs. The seventeenth-century Italian island garden of Isola Bella was originally designed to resemble a floating geometric, stone galleon, with few plantings, drifting across Lake Maggiore. The Bomarzo sculpture garden at Villa Orsini in Lazio, Italy, is a collection of grotesque stone figures and fantastical beasts. Not merely a repository for sculpture, the garden was meant to be interpreted as a series of cryptic allusions to sixteenth-century and classical literature.

Possibly the best example of a modern sculpture garden attached to a city residence can be seen at the Palazzo Venier di Leoni, which belonged to Peggy Guggenheim. Located along the Grand Canal in Venice, Italy, the house is now a museum, filled with her astonishing collection of modern art. In 1982, Italian architect Giorgio Bellavitis designed the adjoining garden to display works of art, including pieces by Max Ernst, Alberto Giacometti, and Claire Falkenstein. Made of masonry and Belgian block, the garden has trees, shrubs, and stone and marble seating.

One doesn't have to have art works of modern or old-master craftsmanship as a reason to create a sculpture garden. Antique shops, galleries, and art schools are a good source for creations. Carvings and constructions of stone, wood, bronze, copper, metal, and even found objects can be used. Sculpture gardens require a minimum of maintenance. The most challenging aspect is selecting the right piece or pieces to fit the sense of place and, most importantly, to fit the scale of the site and to place them decorously.

Most sculpture gardens have hard surfaces. Contrasts can be created by juxtaposing cobbles, pebbles, and gravel with concrete, brick, or tile designs. Unless the seat itself is a specially carved work of art, unobtrusive seating is suggested. Plantings, of course, are optional. A groundcover or a wall overrun with an evergreen vine can be handsome focal points.

COMMUNITY GARDENS

In much of early Western culture, gardens were created and tended communally. Medieval monks and nuns healed and fed themselves with the herbs and edibles that grew in their cloistered gardens. During World War II, civilians worked together to create the celebrated victory garden.

"It can be important for people who move into a neighborhood to become part of the community," says Carrie Maher, director of the Lotus Community Garden in New York City. One way to get to know your neighbors and to meet new people is by joining in the fun of an urban community garden. "In this case, people are sharing in something of beauty. Gardens are social places that seem to form their own 'families.' After all, Adam and Eve, the first couple, met in a garden," says Maher.

In 1982, The Trust for Public Land and luxury condominium developer, Bill Zeckendorf with Ms. Maher created the concept of the 7,000-square-foot (2,130-square meter) Lotus Garden. Residents overlook the garden that sits over the condominium's garage. More than thirty volunteers actively garden there. Open from 8 A.M. to nightfall, access is free to garden participants and building residents.

The garden is a lush oasis in the concrete canyons of Upper Manhattan. There are forty-two trees, shrubs, and vines and more than one hundred perennials growing. There is an herb garden, a rock garden, and a berry patch. A native plant and woodland area has recently been added with shade-loving flowers and ferns. Pathways of oak chips meander throughout the garden, which is decorated with rock ornaments, moss and fungi-covered tree stumps. Several benches provide resting places to contemplate the garden. There are even two ponds, graced with water lilies and lotuses and filled with exotic fish. The diversity of such a community garden illustrates the virtually unlimited design and plant possibilities for the urban setting.

Joining a community garden is a great way to learn gardening, and to meet people.

One of the oldest community gardens in Manhattan, this little slice of Eden is located in Greenwich Village. Although the residents of the area do not tend this garden themselves, they arrange for its design and ongoing maintenance.

CHAPTER FIVE

FINISHING TOUCHES

ORNAMENTS

FURNISHINGS

WATER FEATURES

GARDENING ARTS

THE URBAN WILDLIFE GARDEN

© Ken Druse

ORNAMENTS

Ornamentation can be used either as a focal point or as an accent. The sundial depicted here acts as an eye-catching yet integral focal point in this quaint herb and vegetable garden.

In his book *Room Outside: A New Approach to Garden Design* (Thames Hudson Books: London, 1985), the British landscape architect John Brookes writes, ''Ornamentation should be integrated with the design of the garden, and the accents it provides should not look as if they were applied as an afterthought. . . . Both the scale and the colour of the ornamentation should fit the character of the setting.'' Unless you are deliberately planning an architectural, sculpture garden where plants take second place, ornamentation should be used selectively and sparingly. Ornaments are most effective when they don't dominate the plantings, but rather, are used as focal points. Small-scale ornaments, for example, belong in small gardens, while a well-planned combination of large and small pieces belong in larger spaces.

In elevated gardens, where weight is always a primary consideration, avoid heavy materials such as stone and lead when choosing large statuary and containers. There are a great variety of light-weight replicas that are much more suitable for your conditions. In backyard gardens, where any material can be supported, don't get carried away and choose ornaments that will be out of scale with your garden's design.

Garden-ornament sellers have many items from which to choose. If there aren't any bona-fide garden ornament merchants in your city, many major dealers ship by mail order (see ''Sources and Useful Addresses''). Appropriate selections for city gardens can include small urns and obelisks. There are finials in pineapple, pinecone, and ball shapes as well as carved stone bowls, baskets, and vases of

This wall niche holding a brass vase of hyacinths illustrates one of the many ways that space for special garden ornamentation can be built into a garden's design.

A cobalt-blue urn provides a bright accent in this garden space.

fruits and flowers. Small busts can be placed atop pedestals, while pedestals themselves make very attractive garden ornaments. You can find copies from virtually every period: ancient, Greek, Gothic, Renaissance, baroque, Victorian, art nouveau, Bauhaus, modern, and postmodern.

Mythical creatures such as gods and beasts also are popular items—a baby unicorn, for example, would enchant children. Turtles, frogs, birds, and armadillos are available in wood, fiberglass, and stone, while an Oriental foo dog comes in various materials. There are many lovely hand-painted ceramics from Italy, Spain, and Portugal (which would have to be brought indoors in cold climates). Lion heads and fox heads fashioned out of stone, rosette- and vegetal-patterned plaques, sun dials, and faces of the sun or moon can be mounted on exterior walls.

To please your artistic sensibilities, create a landscaped corner for a special sculpture, or search for just the right piece to ornament a planting area. Modern sculpture can be commissioned or purchased in an art gallery. Period garden sculptures are often sold at auction houses, and with a little imagination, one can find an endless array of objects at flea markets, country auctions, and antiques shops.

Your garden should delight all the senses, and the value of sound shouldn't be ignored. To take advantage of every aspect of nature in adding ornamentation, hang wind chimes or copper or bronze Chinese bells, which will provide soothing music at all times of day. Wall fountains, too, with recirculating pumps powered by electricity produce the tranquil resonance of gurgling water.

FURNISHINGS

This unfinished bench contributes an orderly yet informal feeling to this urban garden corner.

Evoking the charm of the Old South, recreations of antique wrought-iron furniture are particularly suitable for city gardens in that region.

Above : It is difficult to believe that this lush, comfortable garden, whose style hints at Mexico and the Caribbean, exists on a city terrace in a northern city.

Garden furnishings include chairs, benches, stools, and tables. Furnishings should harmonize with the design scheme, rather than glaringly stand out. Woody, natural colors blend in while white furniture attracts attention to itself. To avoid letting the furniture become the centerpiece of the garden, place it near trees, which also provide welcome shade on a hot, sunny day.

Garden furniture can be formal or informal. The formal sort looks rather like traditional interior furnishings. The lines are crisp and elegant, with backs, arms, and legs which are carved or decorative. Benches are often modeled after the classical designs of the ancient world. Informal furniture has a relaxed, country feeling to it. Old chairs can be hand painted in the country style with hearts and ducks. Wooden garden furniture is available in an array of regional and rustic designs—rough-hewn and bent-willow seats are particularly attractive and contribute to the garden theme. Another long-forgotten

"seat," is the old-fashioned wooden swing, secured with ropes hanging from a sturdy tree branch and located over a soft carpet of greenery.

Wicker furniture is a common choice, but is good only in warm, dry climates. Painted and rust-proofed wrought-iron pieces are a good choice for city gardens as they are durable and easy to care for. These furnishings are often crafted with lacelike patternings that make them fine decorative features for a city garden. Because they can be left outside all year long, weather-treated redwood, cedar, oak, teak, and mahogany, however, are your best choices for materials. If you choose wooden tables and chairs, cover the chair bottoms with comfortable, waterproof chintz-covered cushions that can be tied on and removed in winter. For elevated gardens, furniture must be heavy enough to withstand winds; it should have an open, slatted design so that wind blows through it. Additionally, outdoor furniture must be easy to clean.

WATER FEATURES

Perhaps more so than in any other type of garden, the use of water in urban gardens has a far-reaching design impact. Water adds an authentic touch of nature to the city environment by nurturing the life that grows within it, whether it is plants, animals, or both. In the same way that contrasting paving, groundcovers, plant forms, and color are used to introduce variety and interest in a small space, water can be used to amplify a garden's effect by introducing diversity. Additionally, the sound of flowing water is very soothing, so you might want to consider installing a fountain. Water's reflective properties, meanwhile, can amplify the effects of greenery and outdoor lighting and mirror the changing face of the sky.

A water feature, therefore, provides great interest in the garden. There are several ways to approach this element. If you have a backyard garden, you may wish to create a small pool. To do so, you can either use a butyl pond liner as a water container if the feature will be small, or, if you prefer a larger feature, you can create a depression of waterproof concrete. Deeper ponds must be reinforced with extra base material, such as steel mesh. Prefabricated fiberglass growing pools are also available; they require sturdy PVC liners. Pools can be put into the ground and surrounded with stone or set into a lightweight wooden frame on your terrace.

Whatever method you choose, aquatic plants can be grown in open baskets filled with potting mix, and bog plants can be planted directly into a mixture of peat and soil, layered onto the pond base. A pump can also be installed to circulate water. Before undertaking such a project, however, make sure that you are not violating any city codes. A landscape architect could also provide sound advice and guidance.

There are a variety of stunning plants that can add charm to your water garden.

Courtesy Morgan Wheelock Inc. Landscape Architects

© Ken Druse

Above left: This formal lily pond accentuates a view of Boston Harbor. Notice that the aquatic flowers are white, in keeping with the overall color scheme of the design. Designed by Morgan Wheelock. **Above right:** A modern water feature acts as both fountain and sculpture. Even its color blends richly with the purple and lavendar cineraria and campanula behind it.

Water lilies, lotuses, and bog plants, which require three to five hours of sunshine a day, add immeasurably to the appeal of a small pool. In the evening, some species of night-blooming water lilies can be indirectly lit for a spectacular effect. Water lilies need 10 to 18 inches (25 to 50 centimeters) of still water to grow. The leaves of water lilies help prevent the growth of algae. Bog plants, including dwarf papyrus, Chinese water chestnuts, and bog lilies, require extremely moist soil. Marginal aquatics need about 3 inches (7.5 centimeters) of water, while submerged aquatics thrive on about 12 inches (30 centimeters) of water. Marginal aquatics include the water forget-me-not (Myosotis scorpioides), which boasts delicate flowers, and brooklime (Veronica bec-cabunga), whose flowers and foliage are equally delightful. A pond or small pool needs to be oxygenated to sustain life, and you should include plants that perform this function. Among them are the submerged aquatics waterweed (Egeria densa) and curled pondweed (Potamogeton crispus).

If your backyard space is simply too small, or if your urban garden is on a terrace or rooftop, another option is to use a whiskey half-barrel lined with durable PVC covering as a miniature water garden. You can fit two small water lilies, two bog plants, or one of each in the barrel. Other possibilites include birdbaths, oversized urns filled with aquatic plants, and small-scale waterfall systems of water jets and skillfully placed rocks.

GARDENING ARTS

© Alex Roy

© R.W. Kosturko

Bonsai

Bonsai ranks among the most demanding of garden arts requiring a skillful hand and a full understanding of the technique. Bonsai, derived from the ancient Chinese art of dwarfing trees and shurbs in containers, was adapted several hundred years ago by the Japanese. In the Western world, however, where many native species have been found suitable for bonsai, the technique has an enthusiastic following. Horticultural societies often host lectures on the art, and botanical gardens periodically offer hands-on-classes.

Plants grown in true bonsai manner are usually classified into two specific groups—trees or grasses. The larger group, trees, consists of pines and oaks, foliage trees (such as the Japanese ma-

ple), fruit trees (like persimmon or crabapple), and flowering trees (such as cherry or plum). Grass bonsai consists of shrubs, mosses, and bamboo.

Bonsai is an art form and its cultivator a bonsai artist. These dwarfed container-grown plants must be "trained" first, perhaps for decades, by regular pruning, feeding, and watering, and by applying wire coils, which are used to restrict the plant's growth, to the plant's branches. Once coaxed into the desired shape, the plant is then maintained and cared for—sometimes for generations.

The bonsai's shape may be intentionally contorted or allowed to assume the natural shape of its larger counterpart. As a container plant, it works well as a meaningful architectural feature when placed by a door or at the corner of a terrace or garden walk. The bonsai is undoubtedly a revered, living work of art that should be

valued for its development, composition, and beauty.

Topiary

While the technique of restricting a plant's size by pruning and potting is an art form that originated in the Orient, topiary—the art of geometrically designing plants to change their natural shape—is essentially a Western practice. Topiary is particularly well-suited to formal city gardens. One should be careful, however, not to turn a beautifully designed garden into an overdone menagerie of sculpted animals.

THE URBAN WILDLIFE GARDEN

Far left: *The art of bonsai requires great skill and knowledge on the part of the gardener; it is an expensive but rewarding hobby.* **Left:** *This topiary display is obviously on a scale that is much too large for an urban garden. Nevertheless, smaller topiary can lend dignity and grace to a formal city garden.*

Imagine a garden for meditating surrounded by monarch butterflies fluttering around gaillardia (*Gaillardia* spp.) or chickadees refreshing themselves in a Victorian birdbath on your terrace. Picture the curious child's amazement at first sight of a spring wren or his or her excitement over caterpillars and adult swallowtails in July. Wildlife provides a wonderful educational experience, helps your garden grow, and enhances the appeal of it to visitors.

By providing the proper devices for wildlife, you can attract fascinating creatures to your city garden. You'll soon discover that red flowers attract hummingbirds, bellflowers attract bumblebees, and bright orange and pink flowers attract butterflies—it's easy to become an amateur naturalist in your own urban space. According to Violet Stevenson in her book *The Wild Garden* (Viking: New York, 1985), one advantage to attracting wildlife to your garden is the automatic ecosystem of nature. If your garden attracts one kind of animal, it will inevitably attract another. For example, if your garden plants are attacked by *aphids*, which suck valuable juices from plants, visiting birds or ladybugs and other insects will consume the problems for their nourishment. *Syrphids*, banded yellow-and-black insects, whose larvae love to gorge on aphids, can be welcome guests.

Water is the most important ingredient in a wildlife garden. Any size container will do—a saucer sunk into a flower border, a traditional birdbath, or a garden pond filled with radiant water lilies. While water brings birds and other beautiful wildlife to your garden, it also attracts insects. This same water will, in turn, bring delicate dragonflies in summer to lunch on the more bothersome insects in your pond. One of these undesirable visitors is the mosquito. In as little as two weeks, it can have laid eggs, which will have grown to mature adults. By frequently replacing the water in your pool, you can halt the life cycle

Primarily used in landscape gardening, topiary is usually composed from thick, slow-growing evergreens such as box and yew, arborvitae and privet. The sculptures themselves can be as elaborate or as simple as you please. Some trees and shrubs are designed to resemble statuary (such as birds, nymphs, or urns) and intricate mazes, while others are clipped into simple cubes and obelisks. Parents looking forward to playing outside with their children might consider some small-scale topiaries. Little rabbits, ducks, and elephants shaped out of green leaves can be grown on wire forms specifically designed for the purpose. Topiary should be set off on its own or it can be planted against a simple background where it can be appreciated and enjoyed. The center of a lawn, near an entrance or pathway, or by a fence or wall, are all ideal spots for garden topiary.

Select plants, such as crocuses, will attract beneficial insects like the bumblebee.

before completion. In John V. Denniss's *The Wildlife Gardener* (Knopf, 1985), he suggests introducing the mosquito fish (*Gambusia affinis*) in larger reflecting pools to combat this problem.

There is no reason a terrace gardener cannot lure the common Eastern Phoebe, among others, with the proper birdfeeder. Most birds require these basic needs: food, water, and shelter. Birdhouses can make up for the lack of old oak trees for nesting birds on rooftop gardens. Bird watchers can view early morning feeders from a safe distance at their carefully chosen sitting area. Feeders filled with a combination of wild bird feed and suet will provide your flock with their basic dietary needs. Oranges are an inexpensive food source for birds. Don't leave food uneaten for long, however, or it will attract night stalkers such as racoons, oppossums, and rats. This can cause disease within your bird population.

Plants with berries, such as elderberries, attract birds by providing a source of food. The honeysuckle vine feeds birds in au-

tumn and calls hummingbirds with trumpet blooms in summer.

The common gray squirrel will be the most predominant form of wildlife to appear. Squirrels actually favor mushrooms, oranges, apples, and grapes for their diets. Recycle your leftover scraps for them—the more decayed the better. Squirrels will not eat suet and will stay away from a bird's nest, but take care with how you place your seed because the gray squirrel will find a way to it. Suspending the container on a limb or extension 8 to 10 feet (2.4 to 3 meters) from a wall or tree will convince them to keep off. Cats, as well, can be prevented from climbing post feeders by attaching an inverted funnel-shaped metal collar at the base. This should be placed 3 to 4 feet (.9 to 1.2 meters) from the ground to deter any further scampering upward. Also, your feline should wear a bell around the neck to warn the birds of the approaching predator. Domestic pets may try to nibble on your carefully chosen plants. You can try spraying hot salsa as a remedy against

their discriminating palate. Or plant your cat's own crop of oat grass to chew upon.

A window box (see page 36) can provide a rest stop for butterflies. Butterflies, and the flowers they land upon, will need at least four to six hours of sunlight to flourish. These beautiful winged creatures are attracted to warm colors: oranges, pinks, reds, and yellows. Butterflies are a sign of tranquility in nature—floating along softly from flower to flower. Plant your garden spot along a protected hedge, fence, or corner wall away from wind swirls to encourage butterflies to linger. Nectar is a source of energy for the butterfly. The plants listed on page 79 are full of this sweet sap and convince butterflies to return often. The Mexican sunflower (*Tithonia rotundifolia*) is a favorite of the monarch. A tall, heat-resistant red daisy, it will bloom all summer long. Wildflowers, such as milkweed, sweet clover, and chicory are bringing butterflies back to urban centers. As new trends are incorporated into contemporary garden designs, these splendid creatures of nature increasingly appear.

© Ken Druse

Plants like joe-pye-weed can attract the beautiful swallowtail butterfly to your sanctuary in the city.

Butterfly Plants

Plant	Butterfly
Aster (*Aster* 'Ostrich Plume')	Tortoiseshell
Bachelor's Button (*Centaurea* spp.)	Red Admiral
Butterfly bush (*Buddleia* spp.)	Fritillary
Butterfly weed (*Asclepias tuberosa*)	Edward's hairstreak
Globe amaranth (*Gomphrena* spp.)	Snout
Globe thistle (*Echinops* spp.)	Painted lady
Milkweed (*Aslepias* spp.)	Monarch
Nasturtium (*Tropaeolum* spp.)	Common sulphur
Snapdragon (*Antirrhinum* spp.)	Buckeye
Queen Anne's lace (*Daucus carota*)	Black swallowtail
Violet (*Viola* spp.)	Great-spangled fritillary
Zinnia (*Zinnia* spp.)	Yellow-tiger swallowtail

Other Butterfly Plants

Annuals	Perennials
Cosmos (*Cosmos* spp.)	*Coral bell* (Hevchera sanguinea)
Gaillardia (*Gaillardia* spp.)	Coreopsis (*Coreopsis* spp.)
Lantana (*Lantana* spp.)	Dahlia (*Dahlia* spp.)
	Daylily (*Hemerocallis* spp.)
	Liatris (*Liatris* spp.)
	Phlox (*Phlox* spp.)

Container Plants for Birds

Latin Name	Common Name
Nadina var. 'Nana Purpurea'	Boston ivy
Pyracantha var. 'Tiny Tim'	Compact inkbery
Ilex crenata var. 'Helleri'	Chinese sacred bamboo
Ilex glabra compacta	Firethorn
Ilex opaca var. 'Maryland Dwarf'	
Parthenocissus tricuspidata	Maryland American holly
	Heller Japanese holly

Bird Feed

Bird	Feed
Blue Jay	Sunflower
Cardinal	Safflower seeds
Catbird	Chopped fruit
Chickadee	Sunflower hearts
Finch	Black oil sunflower
Mockingbird	Suet (beef or mutton fat)
Morning dove	Finely chopped corn
Robin	Chopped fruit
Sparrow	Millet (white)
Woodpecker	Suet

Hummingbird Plants

Common Name	Latin Name
Annual delphinium	*Delphinium* spp.
Balloon flower	*Platycodon*
Beard-tongue	*Penstemon* spp.
Beebalm	*Monarda* 'Cambridge Scarlet'
Red cardinal flower	*Lobelia cardinalis*
Russell hybrids	*Lupinus* spp.
Salvia 'Rodeo'	*Salvia* spp.
Snapdragon	*Antirrhinum* spp.
Spider flower	*Cleome*
Tobacco plant	*Nicotiana* spp.

Bumblebee Plants

Common Name	Latin Name
Apple blossom	*Malus* spp.
Canadian goldenrod	*Solidago canadensis*
Foxglove	*Digitalis purpurea*
Live Forever	*Sedum* 'Autumn Joy'
Sage	*Salvia officinalis*
Virginia bluebells	*Mertensia virginica*
Yarrow	*Achillea millefolium*

PLANT GROWTH CHARTS

N O R T H E A S T

	NAME	ZONE	MAXIMUM HEIGHT	OPTIMUM SUN EXPOSURE	COMMENTS
	SHELTERED				
TREES	Flowering Dogwood *Cornus florida* 'New Hampshire'	5	20 ft	all	deciduous; full burst of flowers in spring; brilliant scarlet color in autumn; berries attract birds
	Japanese Crabapple *Malus floribunda*	5	20 ft	all	deciduous; pyramidal shape; excellent for small spaces
	Weeping Japanese Pagoda *Sophora japonica* 'Pendula'	5	20-30 ft	E, S	deciduous; long bloom period; tolerates wind and ice
	Scarlet Japanese Maple *Acer palmatum* 'Sanguineum'	5	20 ft	all	deciduous; use in shade gardens and Oriental designs
SHRUBS	Lily-of-the-Valley *Pieris japonica* 'Valley Valentine'	6	9 ft	all	evergreen; use in Oriental designs; shade gardens
	Dwarf Fothergilla *Fothergilla gardenii* 'Blue Mist'	5	3 ft	S, W	native to Northeast; white spring flowers; mixes well with conifers
	Fountain Bush *Buddleia altenifolia*	5	12 ft	S, W	deciduous; prune after bloom period; purple flowers
	Summersweet *Clethra alnifolia* 'Pink Spire'	5	10 ft	S, W	native to Northeast; suited to dry areas and seashore
PERENNIALS	Astilbe *Astilbe x arendsii* 'Fanal'	5	2-4 ft	N, E	hardy; use in woodland shade gardens; fertilize every summer
	Bellflower *Campanula glomerata*	3	1-3 ft	N, E	hardy; use in rock garden borders and shade gardens
	Foxglove *Digitalis purpurea* 'Foxy'	5	4 ft	E, S	use in cutting and wild gardens; attracts bumblebees
	Garden Phlox *Phlox paniculata* 'Mount Fujiyama'	4	3 ft	E, S	hardy; large pink, white and scarlet flowers; excellent in borders
	Giant Snowdrops *Galanthus elwesii*	4	4-11 in	**E, S**	bulb; white flowers in earliest spring; does well in containers
	Plantain lily *Hosta decorata*	4	2 ft	**N, E**	hardy; white flower spikes provide contrast in dark corners
ANNUALS	Blue Laceflower *Trachymene coerulea*		2-3 ft	E, S, W	hardy; grows best in well-drained soil
	Busy Lizzy *Impatiens wallerana* 'New Guinea'		2 ft	S, W	tender; use in borders, containers, and small boxes or pots
	Tuberous Begonia *Begonia x tuberhybrida*		2 ft	E, S	tender; use in containers and small patio or terrace pots

TERRACE				
NAME	ZONE	MAXIMUM HEIGHT	OPTIMUM SUN EXPOSURE	COMMENTS
TREES				
Japanese Maple *Acer palmatum* 'Atropurpureum'	3	20 ft	E, S, W	deciduous; use in Oriental and woodland designs
Sargent Crabapple *Malus sargentii*	3	8 ft	all	deciduous; rose-colored spring flowers
Siberian Dogwood *Cornus alba* 'Sibirica'	3	9 ft	E, S, W	deciduous; bright coral-red spring flowers
Silvery Blue Spruce *Picea pungens* 'Glauca Globosa'	3	2 ft	all	evergreen; use as accent with conifers; good container plant
Spreading Euonymus *Euonymus kiautschovica* 'Manhattan'	6	9 ft	all	deciduous; pollution tolerant; flaming red autumn color
SHRUBS				
Cranberry Cotoneaster *Cotoneaster apiculatus*	5	3 ft	E, S, W	evergreen; use for espaliers and low ledges, and in rock gardens
European Cranberrybush *Viburnum opulus* 'Compactum'	5	4-5 ft	S, W	deciduous; pollution tolerant; berries attract birds
Korean Boxwood *Buxus koreana*	6	5 ft	all	evergreen; excellent for formal gardens or topiary
PERENNIALS				
Bearded Iris *Iris hybrids*	3	2 ft	S, W	hardy; use in containers and borders
Black-Eyed Susan *Rudbeckia fulgida* 'Goldsturm'	4	2½ ft	S, W	hardy; native to North America; good container plant; use for wild-garden or meadow designs
Chinese Wisteria *Wisteria sinensis*	5	4-5 ft	E, S, W	deciduous; perfect for trellises and pergolas; makes an attractive weeping tree
Leather Flower *Clematis jackamnii*	4	15 ft	N, E	deciduous vine; flat, open, purple, white, and rose flowers in summer; roots need cool shade; prune in late winter
ANNUALS				
Purple Loosestrife *Lythrum Salicaria*		3-5 ft	all	hardy; spreads rapidly, so use in containers only or to edge garden pools
Dusty Miller *Senecio cineraria*		2-3 ft	E, S, W	tender; lovely grey-tinged foliage; use for edging or borders
Feverfew *Chrysantemum parthenium* 'Golden Feather'		3 ft	E, S, W	daisy-like flowers; use in beds, borders, and small containers
Floss Flower *Ageratum houstonianum*		1 ft	S, W	tender; small, blueish-purple summer flowers; use as edging, walkways, and borders or in containers
Lobelia *Lobelia erinus*		3-8 in	S, W	hardy; lovely cascading form; use in rock gardens and containers

			EXPOSED		
	NAME	ZONE	MAXIMUM HEIGHT	OPTIMUM SUN EXPOSURE	COMMENTS
TREES	Callerya Pear *Pyrus calleryana* 'Faureri'	5	20 ft	all	deciduous; heat, wind, and pollution tolerant
	English Hawthorne *Crategus monogyna* 'Crimson Cloud'	5	20 ft	all	deciduous; thrives in city conditions; berries attract birds
	Service Berry *Amerlanchier canadensis*	4	20-30 ft	all	deciduous; early spring flowers; berries attract birds
SHRUBS	American Arborvitae *Thuja occidentalis*	3	8 ft	all	evergreen; creates columnar or pyramidal windscreen
	Bush Cinquefoil *Potentilla fructicosa* 'Goldfinger'	2	4 ft	S, W	deciduous; low grower; golden summer flowers; tolerates dryness and extreme cold
	Fringetree *Chionanthus retusus*	6	15 ft	S, W	deciduous; early flowering shrub
	Japanese Barberry *Berberis thunbergii* 'Atropurpurea'	4	2 ft	S, W	deciduous; reddish leaves in winter; drought tolerant
	Bridal Wreath *Spiraea x japonica* 'Little Princess'	6	3-4 ft	S, W	deciduous; small crimson summer flowers
	Witch Hazel *Hamamelis x intermedia* 'Arnold Promise'	4	8 ft	E, S, W	deciduous; yellow blooms in late winter; tolerates moderate pollution
PERENNIALS	Allium *Allium roseum*	5	2 ft	S, W	bulb; rose-pink blooms in late spring
	Lily *Lilium rubrum*	5	4-5 ft	S, W	bulb; pink summer trumpet-shaped flowers
	Queen-Anne's-Lace *Daucus carota*	5	1-3 ft	all	hardy; good choice for wild gardens; attracts bees and butterflies
	Trumpet Honeysuckle *Lonicera sempervirens* 'Dropmore Scarlet'	3	50 ft	S, W	deciduous; winter-hardy into Canada
ANNUALS	Martha Washington Geranium *Pelargonium x domesticum*		1½ ft	E, S, W	tender; pink, red, and white flowers; provides long-lasting summer color; use in borders, containers, and window boxes
	Morning Glory *Ipomoea purpurea*		10 ft	S, W	vine; tolerates hot, summer sun; white, red, and purple flowers
	Nasturtium *Tropaeolum majus*		12 ft	all	tender vine; easily grown from seed; tolerates dry soil; orange edible flowers
	Verbena *Lantana camera* 'Sanguinea'		2 ft	S, W	tender; white and deep-red pompom flowers; use small, decorative pots

S O U T H E A S T

SHELTERED

	NAME	ZONE	MAXIMUM HEIGHT	OPTIMUM SUN EXPOSURE	COMMENTS
TREES	Japanese Dogwood *Cornus florida*	5-9	20 ft	E	deciduous; scarlet summer flowers; use in Oriental designs; berries attract birds
	Japanese Maple *Acer palmatum*	6-9	20 ft	S	deciduous; red autumn color; use in woodland and Oriental designs
	Saucer Magnolia *Magnolia soulangiana*	6-9	20 ft	S	deciduous; mauve spring flowers; likes cool, moist spots
SHRUBS	Chinese Holly *Ilex cornuta* 'Rotunda'	6-10	3 ft	N, E, S	evergreen; compact spreading habit; use as windscreen; berries attract birds
	India Hawthorn *Raphiolepis indica* 'Rosea'	7-10	3 ft	E, S	evergreen; use as windscreen; pink flowers
	Japanese Privet *Ligustrum japonicum*	8-10	6-15 ft	all	evergreen; use as hedge or topiary in formal or Oriental designs
PERENNIALS	Aaron's Beard *Hypericum calycinum*	5-8	1-1½ ft	E, S	hardy groundcover; yellow summer flowers; thrives near garden pools
	Fern *Athyrium spp.*	4-9	6 in-2 ft	N, E	native to North America; use in shade and woodland gardens; many varieties
	Mondo Grass *Ophiopogon japonicus*	6-10	6 in-1 ft	N, E, S	evergreen groundcover; tropical, grassy look; lawn substitute
ANNUALS	Fairy Primrose *Primula malacoides*		1½ ft	E, S	tender; pink and white summer flowers; use in moist, soggy areas
	Forget-me-not *Myosotis sylvatica*		1 ft	E, S	hardy wildflower; use under trees
	Spider Flower *Cleome hasslerna*		4-5 ft	E, S	tender; plant under trees in filtered light

TERRACE

	NAME	ZONE	MAXIMUM HEIGHT	OPTIMUM SUN EXPOSURE	COMMENTS
TREES	Bradford Pear *Pyrus calleryana* 'Bradford'	6	30 ft	E, S, W	deciduous; flaming red autumn color; can use for espalier or topiary
	European Fan Palm *Chamaerops humilis*	9	6 in-1 ft	all	palm; large container plant; tolerates hot, dry conditions
	Pigmy Date Palm *Phoenix roebelenii*	9-10	6 in-1 ft	N, E	palm; container or patio plant; has feathery, light green leaves
SHRUBS	Common Camellia *Camellia japonica*	8	3-5 ft	E, S, W	evergreen; use in Oriental designs or for espaliers; many varieties
	Sweet Viburnum *Viburnum odoratissimum* 'Nanum'	8	6-10 ft	E, S	evergreen; white fragrant spring flowers; year-round foliage color; berries attract birds
	Twisted Juniper *Juniperus chinensis* 'Torulosa'	5-9	10 ft	E, S, W	evergreen; use in isolated space so twisted branches are visible

	NAME	ZONE	MAXIMUM HEIGHT	OPTIMUM SUN EXPOSURE	COMMENTS
PERENNIALS	Confederate Jasmine *Trachelospermunium jasminoides*	9	30 ft	E, S	vine; fragrant; requires a structure for support
	Coral Vine *Antigonon leptopus*	8-10	30 ft	E, S, W	tender tendrils grow on fences, trellises, and trees
	Nippon Lily *Rohdea japonica*	6-10	1-1½ ft	N, E	evergreen; short spike of pale-yellow flowers; container plant; use in shade gardens
ANNUALS	English Daisy *Bellis perennis*		6 in	S, W	tender; white to rose daisy flowers in early summer; use in containers, and as borders
	White Sage *Lantana camara* 'Alba'		4 ft	all	tender; container plant; use in all-white gardens; good container plant; shrub-like plant form
	Sweet Pea *Lathyrus odoratus* 'Mammoth Mixed'		6 ft	E, S, W	tender creeper; very fragrant, color varies in flowers; use as border plant

EXPOSED

	NAME	ZONE	MAXIMUM HEIGHT	OPTIMUM SUN EXPOSURE	COMMENTS
TREES	Cherry Laurel *Prunus caroliniana*	7	10-20 ft	E, S, W	evergreen; pink blooms in spring; prune into compact shape
	Crape Myrtle *Lagerstroemia indica*	7-10	10-20 ft	S, W	deciduous; rosy summer flowers; drought tolerant
	Fringe Tree *Chionanthus virginicus*	5-9	10-20 ft	S, W	deciduous; native to North America; white, late-spring flowers
SHRUBS	Golden Bamboo *Phyllostachya aurea*	8	10 ft	E, S, W	evergreen; use in Oriental designs and near water pools; tolerates moist soils
	Flame-of-the-woods *Ixora coccinea*	10	5-10 ft	E, S	evergreen; tropical; brilliant orange flower; use as container plant, hedge, or windscreen
	Japanese Boxwood *Buxus microphylla japonica*	7-10	3 ft	all	evergreen; use in formal gardens, as a hedge, border plant, or as topiary
	Spiraea *Spiraea x vanhouttei*	5	2-3 ft	E, S, W	deciduous; white summer flowers; can be used as hedge or alone
	Goucher Abelia *Abelia x grandeflora* 'Edward Goucher'	3-9	3-5 ft	E, S, W	semi-deciduous; small pink trumpet-shaped summer flowers
PERENNIALS	Lawn leaf *Dichondra carolinensus*	8-10	6 in	all	groundcover; lawn substitute; very invasive
	Poet's Jasmine *Jasminium officinale*	7-10	30 ft	E, S	evergreen vine; fragrant white flowers; use on arbors and trellises
	Lily-of-the-Nile *Agapanthus africanus*	8-9	1-3 ft	S, W	tender bulb; use as container plant, and in rock gardens
ANNUALS	Black-eyed Susan *Thunbergia alata*		6 ft	S, W	vine; likes heat; good container plant; can be grown in wildflower border
	Morning Glory *Ipomoea alba*		50 ft	S, W	vine; white or violet-blue flowers; likes containers; climbs along walls, trellises, fences
	Lily Turf *Liliope muscari*		1-1½ ft	N, E, S	evergreen; use as a groundcover or border; provides contrasting foliage
	Zephyr Lily *Zephyranthes grandiflora*		1 ft	S, W	tender bulb; use in rock gardens, borders, and containers
	Ten-weeks Stock *Matthiola incana* 'Annua'		2 ft	E, S, W	hardy; mix with foxglove, and larkspur in English cottage flower designs

N O R T H W E S T

SHELTERED

	NAME	ZONE	MAXIMUM HEIGHT	OPTIMUM SUN EXPOSURE	COMMENTS
TREES	Amur Maple *Acer ginnala*	5	20 ft	all	deciduous; vibrant scarlet autumn foliage
	Mountain Stewartia *Stewartia ovata*	7	15 ft	E, S	deciduous; white blooms in summer; likes moist acidic soil
	Saucer Magnolia *Magnolia x soulangiana*	2	25 ft	all	deciduous; white flowers in early spring; use in a corner or as a focal point
SHRUBS	Flowering Fuchsia *Fuchsia x hybrida*	4	4-12 ft	N, E, S	deciduous; use as topiary, in a container, or as a hanging plant
	Golden Chaintree *Laburnum x watereri* 'Vossii'	2	25 ft	N, E, S	deciduous; long golden flower clusters in midspring; requires moist soil; good espalier plant
	Red-flowering Currant *Ribes sanguineum*	6	12 ft	E, S, W	deciduous; yields lovely red flowers in spring; berries attract birds
	Tartarian Honeysuckle *Lonicera tatarica* 'Arnold Red'	1	9 ft	all	deciduous; tolerates shade; use as windbreak; thrives in Rocky Mountain region
	Arrowwood *Viburnum davidii*	7	3 ft	N, E, S	evergreen; use as groundcover or grow under Azaleas and Rhododendrons
PERENNIALS	Lily-of-the-field *Anemone coronaria*	5	6 in-1½ ft	N, E	bulb; blooms in early spring; open flower form with red and purple petals
	Lupine *Lupinus polyphyllus*	4	2 ft	all	hardy wildflower; native to North America; best in moist areas; use in wild-garden designs
	Peach-leafed Bells 'Alba' *Campanula persicifolia*	2	3 ft	N, E, W	hardy; use in borders and to lighten dark areas
ANNUALS	Beard-tongue *Penstemon gloxinoides* 'Scarlet and White'		2-3 ft	E, S	half-hardy; prefers cool weather; use in beds or borders; good cutting flower
	Prairie Gentian *Eustoma grandiflorum*		2-3 ft	E, S, W	half-hardy; use in moist soils; good choice for wild gardens
	Blue Wings *Torenia fournieri*		1 ft	E, S	tender; use in moist soils; good for rock gardens

TERRACE

	NAME	ZONE	MAXIMUM HEIGHT	OPTIMUM SUN EXPOSURE	COMMENTS
TREES	European White Birch *Betula pendula* 'Dwarf'	2	3 ft	all	deciduous; striking white peeling bark with weeping branch form
	Fragrant Snowball *Styrax obassia*	5	25 ft	E, S, W	deciduous; fragrant white flowers; use in Oriental designs
	Vine Maple *Acer circinatum*	6	5-30 ft	all	deciduous; fire-red autumn foliage; likes shade; good espalier plant; grows well in British Columbia
	Western Redbud *Cercis occidentalis*	2	1½ ft	E, S, W	deciduous; drought tolerant; brilliant-rose spring flowers

	NAME	ZONE	MAXIMUM HEIGHT	OPTIMUM SUN EXPOSURE	COMMENTS
SHRUBS	Oregon Holly-grape *Mahonia Aquifolium* 'Moseri'	5	3 ft	all	evergreen; fragrant yellow flowers; tolerates wind and sun exposure
	Noble Fir *Abies procera* 'Prostrata'	5	3 ft	all	evergreen; foliage is blue-gray in color; contributes winter beauty with graceful, spreading form
	Scotch Broom *Cytisus scoparius*	4	5-10 ft	E, S, W	evergreen; grow in containers to keep plant from spreading; prune after blooming
PERENNIALS	Pineapple Lily *Eucomis comosa*	7	1-2 ft	all	bulb; blooms in summer; tall greenish-white flower; good for cutting
	Spring Heath *Erica carnea* 'Spring Wood'	2	8 in	E, S	groundcover; blooms in spring; flower color varies; rock garden plant
	Red-Hot Poker *Kniphofia Uvaria*	7	3 ft	S, W	plant in sheltered spot; avoid windy, northern exposures; orange-yellow flowers on tall spikes
ANNUALS	Farewell-to-Spring *Clarkia amoena*		3 ft	S, W	annual; grows well in British Columbia; thrives in crowded conditions
	Sweet Pea *Lathyrus spp.*		3 ft	E, S, W	hardy; use in containers or small terrace boxes
	Tricolor Chrysanthemums *Chrysanthemum carinatum*		3 ft	E, S, W	hardy; use in beds and borders; flowers are bronze, yellow, or crimson

EXPOSED

	NAME	ZONE	MAXIMUM HEIGHT	OPTIMUM SUN EXPOSURE	COMMENTS
TREES	Flowering Plum *Prunus x blireiana*	2	25 ft	E, S, W	deciduous; vibrant pink spring flowers; tolerates city climates
	Japanese Flowering Crabapple *Malus floribunda* 'Profusion'	2	25 ft	all	deciduous; resistant to rust disease; fruit attracts birds
	Russian Hawthorn *Crataegus ambigua*	2	20 ft	S, W	deciduous; extremely hardy; berries attract birds
SHRUBS	Chinese Witch Hazel *Hammamelis mollis*	4	10 ft	all	deciduous; fragrant yellow late-winter flowers
	Common Lilac *Syringa vulgaris*	1	15 ft	all	deciduous; fragrant purple blooms; thrives in Rocky Mountain region
	Flowering Quince *Chaenomeles japonica*	1	2-6 ft	S, W	deciduous; thrives in Rocky Mountain region; excellent as windscreen or hedge; flowers attract hummingbirds
PERENNIALS	Butterfly Weed *Asclepias tuberosa*	4	3 ft	S, W	hardy; orange blooms in summer; mix with grasses and use in wild-garden designs; attracts bees and butterflies
	Pacific Coast Iris *Iris tenax*	4	1 ft	E, S, W	use in rock gardens and borders
	Purple Cornflower *Echinacea purpurea*	all	4 ft	all	mix with daisy forms or with matching colors; has noninvasive root system
ANNUALS	Blue Marguerite *Felicia amelloides*		3 ft	E, S, W	half-hardy; use in well-drained soils; good for borders or for cutting
	Garden Verbena *Verbena x hybrida* 'Pink Bouquet'		1 ft	E, S, W	tender; use in beds and borders or small individual decorative pots

S O U T H W E S T

		SHELTERED			
	NAME	ZONE	MAXIMUM HEIGHT	OPTIMUM SUN EXPOSURE	COMMENTS
TREES	Citrus Trees *Citrus spp.*	8	varies	E	evergreen; fragrant flowers and fruit; good container, espalier, and topiary plant
	Mexican Redbud *Cercis canadensis* 'Mexicana'	5	10 ft	N, E	deciduous; bursting, pink, spring flowers
	Juniper *Juniperus scopulorum* 'Tolleson's Weeping'	4	15 ft	E, S	evergreen; blue foliage; use in Oriental designs
SHRUBS	Agave *Agave spp.*	9	4 ft	S, W	evergreen; succulent; use in rock gardens or desert designs
	Bamboo *Bambusa glancescens Riviereorum*	9-10	10 ft	E, S, E	evergreen; use in Oriental and water-garden designs; grassy leaf form
	Japanese Aralia *Fatsia japonica*	9-10	15 ft	N, E	tropical evergreen; use in containers or as filler at tree base
	Mexican Stone Pine *Pinus cembroides*	7	25 ft	all	evergreen; use in Japanese designs
	Persian Lilac *Syringa x persia*	5	5 ft	S, W	deciduous; fragrant purple flowers
	Chinese Wax-leaf Privet *Ligustrum lucidum*	8	6-25 ft	E	evergreen; use as hedge, windscreen, or topiary
	Arrowwood *Viburnum x burkwoodii*	5-7	4-6 ft	N, E	evergreen; fragrant pinkish-white, tubular spring flowers
PERENNIALS	Aralia Ivy *Fatshedera lizei*	7	8 ft	N, E	evergreen vine; lush greenery creates attractive espalier and wallclimbing designs
	Creeping Fig *Ficus pumila*	8	varies	N, E	evergreen vine; has invasive root system; use for espalier
	Daylily *Hemerocallis spp.*	all	2-3 ft	E, S	hardy; summer blooms; varied colors; fragrant cutting plant; edible flowers
	Umbrella Sedge *Cyperus alternifolius*	7	3 ft	E	tropical evergreen; use in Oriental designs; grows well near water in moist soil
ANNUALS	Calendula Marigold *Calendula officinalis* 'Orange Coronet'		1½ ft	E, S, W	hardy; prefers cool areas; provides long-lasting, bright-orange flowers
	Cape Marigold *Dimorphotheca pluvialis*		1½ ft	S, W	tender; showy blooms; use in well-drained soil
	Carnation *Dianthus barbatus* 'Sweet William'		2 ft	N, E, S	hardy; thrives in sun and shade; good choice for borders and English-cottage designs
	Rocket Larkspur *Consolida ambigua*		2 ft	N, E, S	hardy; excellent bedding plant; can also be supported against ornamental fence

TERRACE				
NAME	ZONE	MAXIMUM HEIGHT	OPTIMUM SUN EXPOSURE	COMMENTS
TREES				
Mock Orange *Prunus caroliniana*	7	20 ft	E, S	evergreen; use in formal designs and as hedge, windscreen, or espalier
Peach Tree *Prunus persica*	5	15 ft	S, W	deciduous; provides bright mass of color in spring; pink, puffy flowers
Weeping Fig *Ficus benjamina*	9	20 ft	S	evergreen; prune into topiary or natural weeping form
SHRUBS				
Gardenia *Gardenia jasminoides*	9-10	6 ft	E, S	evergreen; fragrant, white flowers; use as windscreen
Chinese Hibiscus *Hibiscus rosa-sinensis*	9	5 ft	S, W	evergreen; use as hedge, espalier, or windscreen; attracts hummingbirds
Willow Pittosporum *Pittosporum phillyraeoides*	8	15 ft	all	evergreen; adapts to small spaces; provides grassy effect
Cape Leadwort *Plumbago auriculata*	9	3-4 ft	S, W	evergreen; blue flowers; use as container, espalier, trellis, or pergola plant
Sago Palm *Cycas revoluta*	9	10 ft	E	tropical evergreen; requires no maintenance
PERENNIALS				
Confederate Jasmine *Trachelospermum jasminoides*	8	30 ft	E, S	vine; requires support; fragrant blooms; grow hanging over ledge
Ground Morning Glory *Convolvulus mauritanicus*	7	1 ft	all	evergreen groundcover; blue-gray foliage and flowers; use in rock garden or in baskets
Rosemary *Rosemarinus officinalis*	6	2 ft	S, W	evergreen groundcover; berries attract birds
ANNUALS				
Star Phlox *Phlox drummondii* 'Twinkle'		1½ ft	E, S, W	hardy; use in borders or containers
Garden Petunia *Petunia x hybrida* 'Flash Series'		1½ ft	E, S, W	half-hardy; use in containers or borders
Mexican Zinnia *Zinnia haageana*		1½ ft	E, S	tender; excellent cutting flower, but strip off leaves first
Sweet Alyssum *Lobularia maritima* 'Rosie O'Day'		9 in-1 ft	E	hardy; good edging plant; use in rock gardens

EXPOSED				
NAME	ZONE	MAXIMUM HEIGHT	OPTIMUM SUN EXPOSURE	COMMENTS
TREES				
Crape Myrtle *Lagerstroemia indica*	7	10-20 ft	S, W	deciduous; magenta summer flowers; drought tolerant
Fringe Tree *Chionanthus virginicus*	5	10-20 ft	S, W	deciduous; native to North America; late-spring, white flowers
Italian Cypress *Cypressus arizonica* 'Glauca'	7	40 ft	all	evergreen; silvery-gray foliage; columnar form; use in formal designs or as windbreak
SHRUBS				
Crimson Bottlebrush *Callistemon citrinus* 'Jeffers'	8	6 ft	W	evergreen; use for topiary; spectacular spring red brush blooms
Prickly Pear *Opuntia spp.*	6-10	2-20 ft	S, W	cactus; excellent for erosion control, as windscreen, or in desert designs

	Plant	Zones	Height	Exposure	Notes
SHRUBS	Fan Palm *Chamaerops humilis*	8-10	6 ft	S, W	tropical evergreen; use in narrow areas or as bold accent plant
	Oleander *Nerium oleander*	7	5 ft	S, W	evergreen; likes heat; use as hedge or windscreen
	Red Grassy Yucca *Hesperaloe parviflora*	8	3-4 ft	S, W	evergreen; succulent; has tall red spike blooms; use in rock gardens or borders; thrives in desert conditions
	Spanish Bayonet *Yucca spp.*	6-10	4-25 ft	all	evergreen; succulent; dramatic form; container or border plant
PERENNIALS	Bougainvillea *Bougainvillea spp.*	9-10	varies	S, W	vine; purple, red, and white flowers; use on trellis or pergola or as espalier
	Tickseed *Coreopsis grandiflora* 'Goldfink'	7	2 ft	S, W	hardy wildflower; has yellow blooms; blooms from spring through autumn; use as border or in wild-garden designs
	Gaillardia *Gaillardia grandiflora*	6	1-2 ft	S, W	hardy; red and yellow flowers in spring through summer; tolerates heat; attracts butterflies
	Mexican Primrose *Oenothera berlandieri*	7-10	6 in	all	hardy wildflower; pink and white flowers from April through May; use in rock gardens or for lining walkways
	Pampas Grass *Cortaderia selloana*	8	4 ft	S, W	hardy grass; plant along water creates seaside effect; drought tolerant
ANNUALS	Cosmos *Cosmos sulphureus*		3 ft	S, W	tender; orange, pink, and yellow flowers from July through October; attracts butterflies
	Globe Amaranth *Gomphrena globosa*		2 ft	S, W	hardy; pink and purple flowers from June through October; use as cutting flower; also good for drying
	California Poppy *Eschschozia californica*		1 ft	S, W	wildflower; yellow and orange cup-shaped flowers from spring through summer; use for wild-garden designs or borders

NORTHEAST	ZONES
Portland, Maine	4
Boston, Massachusetts	5
New York, New York	6
Philadelphia, Pennsylvania	6
Detroit, Michigan	4

SOUTHEAST	ZONES
Washington, District of Columbia	7
Nashville, Tennessee	7
Atlanta, Georgia	8
New Orleans, Louisiana	9
Miami, Florida	10
Houston, Texas	9
Dallas, Texas	8

NORTHWEST	ZONES
Portland, Oregon	7
Seattle, Washington	8
Denver, Colorado	4
Salt Lake City, Utah	4
Billings, Montana	3

SOUTHWEST	ZONES
San Francisco, California	9
Los Angeles, California	9
San Diego, California	9
Phoenix, Arizona	8
Tucson, Arizona	9
Albuquerque, New Mexico	6
Tulsa, Oklahoma	6

MIDWEST	ZONES
Omaha, Nebraska	4
Milwaukee, Wisconsin	4
Chicago, Illinois	4
Minneapolis, Minnesota	3

CANADA	ZONES
St. John's, Newfoundland	5
Halifax, Nova Scotia	4
St. John, New Brunswick	3
Montreal, Quebec	3
Toronto, Ontario	3
Winnipeg, Manitoba	2
Regina, Saskatchewan	3
Calgary, Alberta	3
Vancouver, British Columbia	8

SOURCES

DESIGNERS

Ascot Designs
286 Congress Street
Boston, Massachusetts 02210

Grass Roots Garden
75 University Place
New York, New York 10003

Hans Van Zelst
Hans Van Zelst Associates
5 East 73rd Street
New York, New York 10021
—lighting and irrigation design

Maher and Greenwald
Designers of Fine Gardens
241 West 97th Street, PH 2
New York, New York 10025

Morgan Wheelock Inc.
286 Congress Street
Boston, Massachusetts 02210

Nightscaping
A Division of Loran, Inc.
1705 East Colton Avenue
Redlands, California 92373

Reed Brothers
6006 Gravenstein Highway
Cotati, California 94928

Janet Rosenberg and Associates
Landscape Architects, Inc.
28 Cecil Street
Toronto, Ontario M5T 1N3

GARDEN SUPPLIERS AND NURSERIES

W. Atlee Burpee Co.
Warminster, Pennsylvania 18974

Bear Creek Nursery
P.O. Box 411
Bear Creek Road
Northport, Washington 99157

Kurt Bluemel
2543 Hess Road
Tallston, Maryland 21047
—bamboo, grasses

Bountiful Gardens
5798 Ridgewood Road
Willits, California 95490
—organic heirloom seeds, herbs,
grains, flowers

Chesnut Corporation
622 Airport Road
Menasha, Wisconsin 54942
—garden tools

Clyde Robin Seed Company
P.O. Box 2366
Castro Valley, California 94556

The Cook's Garden
P.O. Box 65
Londonderry, Vermont 05148
—culinary vegetable and herb
seeds

The Country Garden
Box 455A
Route 2
Crivitz, Wisconsin 54114
—cutting flowers

De Giorgi Co., Inc.
Box 413
1409 Third Street
Council Buffs, Iowa 51502
—rare seeds

Florentine Craftsmen
46-24 28th Street
Long Island City, New York 11101
—ornamental sculptures

G.M. Nurseries, Inc.
P.O. Box 824
Holland, Michigan 49423

Gale Nurseries, Inc.
Box 264
1716 School House Road
Gwynedd, Pennsylvania 19436
—period and native plants

Gardena, Inc.
6031 Culligan Way
Minnetonka, Minnesota 55345
—tools

Gilbertie's Herb Gardens
Sylvan Lane
Westport, Connecticut 06880

Girard Nurseries
Box 428
Route 20 East
Geneva, Ohio 44041
—rhododendrons, azaleas

Green Gardens
1280 Good Pasture Island Road
Eugene, Oregon 97401
—rhododendrons, azaleas

Harris Seeds
3670 Buffalo Road
Rochester, New York 14624
and
1155 Harkins Road
Salinas, California 93901

Heath Manufacturing
P.O. Box 125
Coopersville, Michigan 49404
—redwood planters

High Altitude Gardens
Ketchum, Idaho 83340
—seeds for alpine gardens

Hilltop Herb Farm
P.O. Box 1734
Cleveland, Texas 77327
—hard-to-find plants

Japan Nurseries
Box 60 M
RD #1
Dey Grove Road
Englishtown, New Jersey 07726
—Japanese garden materials

Lilypons Water Gardens
P.O. Box 10
6800 Lilypons Road
Lilypons, Maryland 21717

Logee's Greenhouses
55 North Street
Danielson, Connecticut 06239
—scented geraniums

Maclin Designs
652 Glenbrook Road
Stamford, Connecticut 06906
—conservatories

Marcolina Brothers, Inc.
Masonry Contractors
133 East Mermaid Lane
Chestnut Hill, Pennsylvania 19118
—lily ponds, waterfalls

McClure and Zimmerman
1422 West Thorndale
Chicago, Illinois 60660
—bulbs

McLaughlin's Seeds
P.O. Box 550
Mead, Washington 99201

Mellinger's, Inc.
3210 W. South Range Road
North Lima, Ohio 44452
—trees

Midwest Wildflower
Box 64
Rockton, Illinois 61072

Milaeger's Gardens
4838 Douglas Avenue
Racine, Wisconsin 53402
—perennials

Moon Mountain
P.O. Box 34
Morro Bay, California 93442

Musser Forests
Box 21RS
Indiana, Pennsylvania 15701
—evergreens, shrubs, azaleas

Natural Gardens
113 Jasper Lane
Oak Ridge, Tennessee 37830

Nature's Garden
Box 488
Route 1
Beaverton, Oregon 47007

Nichols Garden Nursery
1190 North Pacific Highway
Albany, Oregon 97321
—herbs, rare seeds

Nor'East Miniature Roses, Inc.
58 Hammond Street
Rowley, Massachusetts 01969
or
P.O. Box 473
Ontario, California 91762

Oliver Nurseries
1159 Bronson Road
Fairfield, Connecticut 06430
—conifers

Park Seed Co.
Highway 254 North
Greenwood, South Carolina 29647
—flowers, vegetables

Peter's
1320 Route 309
Quakertown, Pennsylvania
—fountains, sundials, planters

Pinetree Garden Seeds
New Gloucester, Maine 04260

Plants of the Southwest
1570 Pacheco Street
Santa Fe, New Mexico 87501

Rhapsis Gardens
Gregory, Texas 78359

Santa Barbara Designs
P.O. Box 90610
Santa Barbara, California 93190

Sculpture Design Imports, Ltd.
416 South Robertson Boulevard
Los Angeles, California 90048

John Scheepers, Inc.
63 Wall Street
New York, New York 10005
—bulbs, perennials

Seed Savers Exchange
P.O. Box 70
Decorah, Iowa 52101

Shanti Bithi Nursery
3047 High Ridge Road
Stamford, Connecticut 06903
—bonsai

Shady Hill Gardens
821 Walnut Street
Batavia, Illinois 60510
—geraniums

Shepherd's Garden Seeds
7389 West Zayante Road
Felton, California 95018
—hard-to-find vegetables, edible
flowers

Smith and Hawken
25 Corte Madera
Mill Valley, California 94941
—garden tools

Sprain Brook Nursery, Inc.
448 Underhill Road
Scarsdale, New York 10583
—shrubs, trees, perennials,
woodland plants

Stark Brothers Nurseries and
 Orchards
Louisiana, Missouri 63353
—fruit and berry trees

Thompson and Morgan
P.O. Box 1308
Jackson, New Jersey 08527
—vegetables and flower seeds

William Tricker, Inc.
P.O. Box 398
74 Allendale Avenue
Saddle River, New Jersey 07458
 and
P.O. Box 7843
7125 Tanglewood Drive
Independence, Ohio 44131
—specializes in water gardens

Vick's Wildgardens, Inc.
Box 11
Conshohocken State Road
Gladwyne, Pennsylvania 19035
—wildflowers, native plants, ferns

Andre Viette
Box 16
Route 1
Fisherville, Virginia 22939
—numerous varieties of hosta

Wayside Gardens
Hodges, South Carolina 29695
—bulbs, perennials

We-Du Nurseries
Box 724
Route 5
Marion, North Carolina 28752
—wildflowers, native plants

White Flower Farm
Litchfield, Connecticut 06759
—perennials, begonias

Williams-Sonoma
P.O. Box 7301
San Francisco, California 94120

Wildginger Woodlands
P.O. Box 1091
Webster, New York 14580
—shrubs, ferns, wild and native
plants

Woodlanders
1128 Colleton Avenue
Aiken, South Carolina 29801

A World Seed Service
P.O. Box 1058
Redwood City, California 94064

Wyatt-Quarles Seed Company
P.O. Box 2131
Raleigh, North Carolina 27602
—herbs

SOURCES FOR FURTHER INFORMATION

Administrative Council
Extension Service
United States Department of
 Agriculture
Washington, D.C. 20250

American Horticultural Society
Department N
PO Box 0105
Mt. Vernon, Virginia 22121

American Rhododendron Society
RD #1 Kresson-Gibbsboro Road
Marlton, New Jersey 08053

American Rock Garden Society
413 Little Egypt Road
Elkton, Maryland 21921

American Rose Society
PO Box 30000
Shreveport, Louisiana 71130

The Herb Society of America
2 Independence Court
Concord, Massachusetts 01742

National Wildflower Research
 Center
2600 FM 973 North
Austin, Texas 78725

New England Wildflower Research
 Society
Garden-in-the-Woods
Hemenway Road
Framingham, Massachusetts 01701

RECOMMENDED READING

Allen, Oliver E. *Gardening with the New Small Plants: The Complete Guide to Growing Dwarf & Miniature Shrubs, Flowers, Trees & Vegetables.* Boston, MA: Houghton Mifflin Company, 1987.

Balston, Michael. *The Well Furnished Garden.* New York: Simon and Schuster, 1986.

Barton, Barbara J. *Gardening By Mail: A Sourcebook.* San Francisco: Tusker Press, 1986.

Bird, Rain. *The Gardener's Palette, The Ultimate Garden Plant Planner.* Garden City, New York: Doubleday and Company, Inc., 1987.

Boyd, Lizzie. *Window Gardens: How to Create Beautiful Windows Indoors and Out.* New York: Clarkson N. Potter, Inc./Publishers, 1985.

Bush, James and Louise Brown. *America's Garden Book.* New York: Charles Scribner's Sons, 1980.

Chamberlin, Susan. *Hedges, Screens and Espaliers.* Tucson: HP Books, 1982.

Ferguson, Nicola. *Right Plant, Right Place.* New York: Summit Books, 1984.

Gessert, Kate Rogers. *The Beautiful Food Garden Encyclopedia of Attractive Food Plants.* New York: Van Nostrand Reinhold Company, 1983.

Harper, Pamela and Frederick McGourty. *Perennials: How to Select, Grow & Enjoy.* Tucson: HP Books, 1985.

Johnson, Hugh. *The Principles of Gardening.* New York: Simon & Schuster, Inc., 1979.

Kinahan, Sonia. *The Overlook Guide to Winter Gardens.* Woodstock, New York: The Overlook Press, 1985.

Lerner, Joel M. *101 Townhouse Garden Designs to Fit Your Personality.* Tucson: HP Books, 1987.

Llewellyn, Roddy. *Little English Backyards.* Topsfield, Mass: Salem House, 1985.

McNelan, Ray and Micheline Ronningen. *Pacific Northwest Guide to Home Gardening.* Portland, OR: Timber Press, 1983.

Moon, Douglas. *Gardening for People (Who Think They Don't Know How).* Sante Fe: John Muir Publications, 1975.

Morris, Edwin T. *The Gardens of China: History, Art and Meanings.* New York: Charles Scribner's Sons, 1983.

Nicholls, Richard E. *Hydroponics Soilless Gardening: The Beginner's Guide to Growing Vegetables, Houseplants, Flowers and Herbs Without Soil.* Philadelphia: Running Press, 1977.

Puma, Joan. *The Complete Urban Gardener.* New York: Harper & Row, Inc., 1985.

Saville, Diana. *The Illustrated Garden Planter.* Harmondsworth, Middlesex, England: Penguin Books, 1986.

Seike, Kiyoshi, Masanoba Kudo, and David H. Engel. *A Japanese Touch for Your Garden.* Tokyo: Kodansha International, Ltd., 1980.

Snodsmith, Ralph. *Tips from the Garden Hotline.* Dallas: Taylor Publishing Company, 1984.

Strong, Roy. *Creating Small Gardens.* New York: Villard Books, 1987.

Wilkinson, Elizabeth and Marjorie Henderson. *The House of Boughs: A Sourcebook of Garden Designs, Structures, and Suppliers.* New York: Viking Penguin, Inc., 1985.

Wyman, Donald. *Wyman's Gardening Encyclopedia.* New York: MacMillan Publishing Company, 1986.

Yang, Linda. *The Terrace Gardener's Handbook.* Beaverton, Oregon: Timber Press, 1982.

INDEX

Quality Printing and Binding By:
Leefung-Asco Printers Ltd
830 Lai Chi Kok Road
Kowloon, Hong Kong